FIGHT
with
COWGIRL SPIRIT

A Memoir

SHARYL SAVER

Fight Like a Cowgirl Press

This memoir is a compilation of Sharyl Saver's emails, CaringBridge posts and guestbook entries from her "cheerleaders."

©Fight Like a Cowgirl Press, LLC. All rights reserved, including the right to reproduce this book or portions thereof.

For information, contact fightlikeacowgirl@gmail.com.

All scripture quotations, unless otherwise indicated, are taken from the Holy Bible, New International Version®, NIV®. Copyright ©1973, 1978, 1984, 2011 by Biblica, Inc.™ Used by permission of Zondervan. All rights reserved worldwide. www.zondervan.com.
The "NIV" and "New International Version" are trademarks registered in the United States Patent and Trademark Office by Biblica, Inc.™

Senior and cheerleading pictures used by permission of David Banks Photography.

Cover Illustration/Design: Liina Lundin

ISBN: 978-061528575

Printed in the United States of America

Net proceeds will be placed in trust for Sharyl's children, with a portion donated to cancer research and the American Academy of Dermatology's Camp Discovery to benefit children with chronic skin conditions, a cause near and dear to Sharyl's heart.

www.fightwithcowgirlspirit.com

For Taylor, Jacob and Abby

Trust in your faith. Sometimes faith and hope are the only way to know that there is light.

I promise you the intensity of your pain will lessen over time. Think of the pain as a scar on your heart that reminds you of the love we shared and the memories we created.

Know that I will ALWAYS be with you in your hearts and in your minds. And, remember, one day we will be together again.

Love,
Mom

Contents

Introduction

Turning Uncertainty into a Positive

A Hug and a Lump | 1
Do You Believe in Miracles??? | 2
Woo-Hoo! I'm Halfway Through!!! | 4
BRCA1 Genetic Test Result | 7
God's Gentle Reminder | 8
Tests, Tests and More Tests | 11
"Oh, I Remember, I'm Radioactive." | 13
Please Excuse My Moodiness | 15
Turning Uncertainty into a Positive | 16
My Liver is a Little Sore Today | 18
Pins and Needles | 19

Fight Like a Girl

Believe and Pray with Me | 21
Freedom and Deliverance from Cancer! | 23
Pesky Little Bugger | 25
Slow Down and Enjoy Life | 27
Letter from Taylor | 29
Thanks, Loréal | 31
Turning the Negative into Positive | 33
Laughing Across Life's Bumpy Roads | 35
Smile and Laugh Often. It Feels Good | 37
Take My Hand. I'll Be There | 39
Praise God. Hip Hip Hooray! | 41
True Companion | 42
Fight Like a Girl | 43
Class of '88—Best Hair | 45

Confessions of a Canser Runner

I Hope You Dance | 48
PARP Inhibitors Offer Hope | 51
My Whining for the Day | 52
God's Healing Power and Grace | 54
Happy Birthday to My Hero | 55
Stay Strong! You Are Not Alone | 56
Daily Yogurt Does a Body Good | 58
Don't Mistake Positivity and Faith for Cockiness | 60
Earth Angels | 62
Confessions of a Canser Runner | 65
On Top of the World, Literally | 68

Cowgirl State of Mind

Survivor Lap Reflections | 71
Relay for Life—A Night of Hope | 73
Cowgirl State of Mind | 77
Rainbows—A Mystical Beauty | 80
10th Annual Caylin Saver Memorial Open | 83
Breast Cancer 101 | 84
So Long, Soda | 88
The Fine Print | 91
Pounding Out Negativity | 93
Hope Does Not Disappoint | 95
Rainbows Comes in Many Shapes and Forms | 99
The Power of Pink | 101
God's Been Good to Me | 106

On My Way to Being a Real Cowgirl

Cheerleaders Never Give Up Hope | 109
God Will Lead Me to the Answer | 113
On My Way to Being a Real Cowgirl | 115

My New Normal | 118
How Many Lives Need to Be Spared? | 120
Assumptions Are Not Fact | 122
Signs of Hope | 125
Thank You for the Prayer Covering | 126
Christmas Blessings and People Rainbows | 127
Each Scar Tells a Story | 130
Yogurt Does My Body Good | 132

I Am a COWGIRL

I Am a COWGIRL. I Am a Fighter. I Am a Survivor. | 134
Progression—The Mother of All Swear Words | 137
Watch and Live | 140
Doing the Rocky Balboa Dance Again | 143
Progression-Free Remission | 146
How's That for Crazing and Amazing? | 147
My Butterfly Story | 150
Optimism Is Good | 154
My Secret Weapons—FAITH, HOPE and LOVE | 156

Cowgirls Dust Themselves Off

Canser Is a Jerk | 161
Sunday Is Coming | 164
When I Look Back | 168
Thank You, Dinner Club | 172
Rock Runners | 174
Cowgirls Dust Themselves Off | 178
Trying My Best to Stay in Cowgirl Spirit | 181
PARP Inhibitors—Prayers Please | 183
A Renewed Attitude and Cowgirl Spirit | 185

A Cowgirl with a Will to Survive

A Cowgirl with a Will to Survive | 187
Laughing and Smiling Again | 193
Happy 40th Birthday to Me | 195
It's Good to Be Back at Work | 198
Wearing My Boots Today | 201
Sounds Like a Challenge to Me | 202

My Cup Overflows

Disappointing News | 207
My Cup Overflows | 210
Promising PET Results | 212
Rest in Peace, Elizabeth Edwards | 213
Moment in Time | 217
Alternate Route to a Cure | 222
The Kindness of Family and Friends | 223
Can I Get a YEEHAW? | 225
Thank You to My Hockey Family | 227
Let's Play Hockey Article | 229

Angels Among Us

There's Always Room for Hope and Miracles | 233
God's Love and Devotion | 235
God Bless to All of You | 236
Home with My Family | 238
Angels Among Us | 239
God's Rainbow Is Coming | 242
Fly to Jesus and Live! | 245

Symbol of Hope | 247

Acknowledgments | 249

Fight with Cowgirl Spirit

I have always wanted to be able to call myself a cowgirl. Cowgirls are a tough breed. They may fall but they always saddle up, hold their heads high and ride on.

I thought you had to live on a ranch and own a horse to call yourself a cowgirl, but I've learned being a cowgirl isn't about where you live, it's a state of mind.

—Sharyl Saver

An Inspirational Story of Faith, Hope and Fighting Cowgirl Spirit

What would you do if faced with a terminal diagnosis? Would you hold strong in your faith? Or, would you lose hope?

When Sharyl Saver, a vibrant young wife and mother, was diagnosed with a recurrence of breast cancer that had spread to her lymph nodes and liver, she chose to hold strong. Powered by unwavering faith and the spirit of a cowgirl, Sharyl dusted herself off, saddled up and fought cancer with incredible courage.

As she battled triple-negative breast cancer, an aggressive form that overwhelmingly strikes young women, Sharyl shared her journey with poignant, honest and, at times, humorous entries on her CaringBridge website. Hundreds followed her story, with visits to the site surpassing 34,000.

Sharyl's uplifting words inspired her readers to dance and believe in the power of prayer, to smile and laugh, to live each day with purpose and to embrace the rain along with the rainbows. In return, she promised to hold her head high and fight like a cowgirl.

Sharyl made it her mission to help change the face of cancer—to let others know that people with cancer can still live productive and healthy lives. She continued to exercise, work and be a wife and mom—a hockey, football, dance, soccer and baseball mom, no less—while receiving chemotherapy, for as long as she could.

On occasion, Sharyl's cowgirl spirit was broken, but her steadfast belief in God and a strong support network always helped restore her faith and cowgirl meters back to full.

We invite you to share Sharyl's journey of faith, hope and fighting cowgirl spirit. You'll sing, laugh, run, dance and pray with her as she encounters challenges and unexpected blessings along the way.

—Sharyl's Posse

Turning Uncertainty into a Positive

A Hug and a Lump

Thursday, April 26, 2007

Last Monday, my son Jacob gave me a hug and put his head on my chest. It was tender where he had laid his head, and when I felt around the area, I discovered a lump. On Wednesday, I decided to go to my doctor and have her check it out. She felt the lump and didn't seem too concerned, but suggested a mammogram and possible ultrasound to be safe.

On Thursday, I had the mammogram and ultrasound, and the doctor thought the lump looked suspicious but said that it was small—1 cm. She ordered a biopsy for the next day. Yesterday, I received the news that I have breast cancer. I don't know anything other than that at this point.

I have an appointment next week with a surgeon to determine my course of action. If I could make a request of my family and friends, it would be to please include me in your prayers. I do believe that because of the tumor's small size—and the fact that it was caught early—that I will be HEALED.

Thank you all for being a part of my life,
Sharyl

Do You Believe in Miracles???

Tuesday, May 22, 2007

Thank you for your kind thoughts and prayers for my healing. I'm recovering very well from the lymph node biopsies and surgery to remove the cancerous tumor.

I've had a lot of doctor's appointments over the last week. First with my surgeon, who explained again that the cancer had not spread to my lymph nodes and my margins were clear (meaning the area around the tumor didn't show any signs of cancer).

However, the grade of the tumor (meaning how quickly the cancer cells grow) was a three out of three. This means the tumor was fast-growing. My surgeon felt that it could have doubled in size in a matter of weeks. She also mentioned that most people don't find tumors as small as mine—1.1 cm.

So, it is with the utmost praise that I say, "THANK YOU, GOD, FOR GIVING ME A HUG VIA JACOB!" Do you believe in miracles???

My surgeon said I had Stage 1 infiltrating ductal carcinoma. Although it is considered an early stage of breast cancer, because of my age and the high grade of the tumor, chemotherapy is recommended to reduce the risk of recurrence. And with faith and chemo, I believe I will be cancer-free forever.

I also met with the oncologist, who explained that I would receive four treatments of one type of chemo and four treatments of another. She then ordered scans of my entire body. I think every inch of my body has been scanned over the last two days! I begin my chemo treatments on Thursday, May 31st, and will go every other week for a total of eight treatments.

I appreciate your invitations to help my family and me and may have to take you up on your offers in the coming months. I'm so grateful to have all of you in my corner in support of my healing and recovery. As always, I welcome your phone calls and visits of encouragement, love and support.

I really don't know how to begin to thank you all for your gestures of kindness and generosity except to maintain a positive attitude and stay strong.

Peace and love,
Sharyl

Woo-Hoo! I'm Halfway Through!!!

Thursday, July 12, 2007

It has been a while since I have sent an update on how I am feeling and how the chemotherapy is going, so I thought it was time...(It's a long one.)

As of this afternoon, I'm finished with the first chemo drug. I actually tolerated chemo very well. I had one bad week, a week after my second round, which in my opinion really was the result of a side effect of a side effect.

I thought I was mentally prepared to relinquish my high-school title of "Best Hair," but on Sunday, June 17th, my hair was combing out in big strands. I knew it had been thinning, so I decided to hold off on washing it. Monday, I washed it and had a lot of hair in my hands by the time I was done. Then I tried to comb it while it was still wet, and it was a very depressing moment. I decided I had to get rid of it.

Compliments of my friend and stylist of many years, Sandy, I made it through the shaving of my head with only welled-up eyes. I played around with hats and wigs for the next few days and tried to avoid mirrors like the plague. I developed a sinus headache and then caught a stomach bug for 36 hours. But by Sunday evening, June 24th, I was feeling like my old self again—minus the boobs and hair.

I'm actually quite comfortable now just wearing an engineer-type baseball hat. And, I've been so comfortable not wearing anything on my head around the house that I've been scaring the neighborhood kids a little when I open the door. I'm working on the title of "The scary lady who lives on the corner."

However, I finally received the blond wig I've been waiting for, and it looks a lot like the short haircut my sister Dianna treated me to before I started chemo in May. I never would have thought I could pull off a short, sassy haircut but I loved it!!! So it shouldn't take me as long to grow my hair back. (I say that now...)

Also, due to the support, research and funding of organizations such as Susan G. Komen for a Cure, scientists have been able to discover two known mutations (BRCA1 and BRCA2) that significantly increase a woman's lifetime risk of breast and ovarian cancers, as well as a very slight increase for men to develop breast and certain other cancers.

At my second chemo treatment, I learned that I carry a mutation in the BRCA1 (breast cancer 1) gene. So, if there was any hesitation in my mind about my decision to have a bilateral mastectomy, after meeting with a cancer geneticist, I no longer have any regrets or uncertainty. The bilateral mastectomy greatly reduces my risk for recurrence.

I will also have my ovaries removed in the near future as they no longer serve a purpose for me and doing so will decrease my risk of ever developing ovarian cancer to about 4%. It also will reduce my risk of breast cancer recurrence. Fortunately, I have responded extremely well to the anti-nausea drugs I get in my IV during chemo and also a drug I take the day of and two days after chemo.

I still exercise four to five days a week (lighter workouts in the week after chemo) and since I don't experience any nausea I am able to eat everything I was able to before I started chemo. I don't know exactly what to expect with the next treatment of Taxol. I know what they tell me, but they also told me that women my age don't tend to do so well during chemo.

This new drug doesn't really have the nausea side effects, but it can cause your bones and joints to ache, and my doctor told me that people who don't get nausea with the drug I am on now tend to experience more aching on Taxol. I am going with the belief that I will tolerate this drug just like I did the last one—very well.

I know your prayers, love, cards and meals are what helped me through the first round, so of course they will help me through the next. I will be done with my chemo on September 6th—just in time to enjoy all the fun of back to school, Jacob's birthday, my sister-in-law Jessie's wedding showers and wedding in October, which we are all in (I think I will borrow my mom's 500cc implants to fill out the dress) and the joyous holidays. My Christmas carol this year will be, "All I want for Christmas are some Double Ds." Just kidding. (I hope to schedule my reconstruction sometime in November and am currently window shopping for the right size.)

I am abundantly blessed to have each one of you in my life. You have all reminded me of the way God brings us love, compassion, generosity and kindness, delivered by family and friends. Your words of encouragement and hope keep me positive and renew my strength. From the depth of my heart and soul, I am forever grateful and thankful for the way each one of you in your own individual way has brightened my days and helped me to find joy and inspiration during this speed bump. (Jason tells me I am a four-wheel drive truck and can cruise right over this speed bump.)

Love and hugs,
Sharyl

P.S. To all the ladies in the crowd, here is my reminder to do your breast self-exams. Feel 'em up girls!

BRCA1 Genetic Test Result

Dear Family,

Attached is a letter, a family tree and the result of my genetic test results that you can bring to your doctor to have him or her write an order for you to have a blood test to determine if you carry the BRCA1 genetic mutation. I believe you have to have the blood drawn through a Cancer Genetics Clinic.

For those of you in Minnesota, I went to through the Health East Care Systems Cancer Genetics Clinic located in St. John's Hospital.

Loréal or Beth, please make copies of this information for your mom. Could someone also pass this information on to Andrea, Loni and Deidre as they are part of this family tree?

I am feeling well and have experienced very minimal side effects from chemo. After Thursday, I will be halfway through my preventive chemotherapy.

Thank you for your love, support and prayers. I know they are helping me to stay healthy and positive.

I love you,
Sharyl

God's Gentle Reminder

*And now these three remain: faith, hope and love
and the greatest of these is love.*
—1 Corinthians 13

Saturday, September 6, 2007

I know I have mentioned to some of you before my feelings on learning I had breast cancer, but I would like to share with all of you that I have never believed God gave me cancer, nor do I believe God allowed me to have cancer.

I do believe God gave me a hug, strategically delivered by my son Jacob, which led me to discover the lump early. God gently reminded me that my mom had breast cancer, my aunt had breast cancer and five of my maternal great grandmother's sisters had breast cancer.

I took those reminders and decided I shouldn't wait until my yearly exam in August to have the lump checked out. And on that note, it is with considerable excitement that I SHOUT, "I am done with chemotherapy and am now in the group that has an 85-90% chance of survival!"

The last chemo drug, Taxol, was very manageable. My eyebrows and eyelashes thinned more, and I did experience some bone and joint pain two to three days after chemo for two to three days. It was usually mild during the day but hurt a little more when I would lie down at night. Nothing a little Vicodin couldn't take care of. Oh, but I could do without the hot flashes.

I'll be returning to work on September 13th and could use a little prayer for my transition back to getting up early, getting the kids and myself ready and everyone off to school, daycare and work with as little screaming as possible. I have gotten quite used to my eight to 10 hours of sleep and very casual dress.

This is where I feel like I'm giving an award speech...

Throughout this experience, first and foremost, I am grateful to God for blessing me with the most amazing man for me in my husband. I know that Jason's love for me has deepened during this journey. He is keeping the promise he made eight years ago of "in sickness and in health." And when he looks at me, I feel as beautiful to him today as the day we married.

I'm also grateful to God for my beautiful children, who love me just because I'm their mommy. For my parents and parents-in-law, whose smiles of joy greeted me the day I got out of surgery and represented the epitome of unconditional love. For my sisters, brother, and sisters- and brothers-in-law who inspire, love and make me laugh.

For my friends who organized dinners and kept my family well fed. To my sister Dianna for doing the Susan G. Komen 3-Day for a Cure breast cancer walk and our Goby's restaurant co-workers and customers, who donated $2,300 for her sponsorship. To my bosom buddy and breast-cancer survivor of one year, Sandy, who lifted my spirits and kept me encouraged.

For my aunts, uncle, cousins, elementary, high school, UMD, softball, US Bank, St. Paul Fire Station 4 B-Shift crew and wives, St. Paul firefighters, St John Vianney Church, daycare friends and all of the other friends I've met in my 37 years, you have reminded me of the precious gift of friendship and the kindness and generosity that goes along with it.

You all have truly defined one of the greatest bible verses, 1 Corinthians 13: *"And now these three remain: faith, hope and love, and the greatest of these is love."*

Surgery and chemotherapy have taught me to become a little less vain, and I have learned that hair and breasts do not define beauty or femininity. I know I am loved by you all not for what I look like on the outside but rather for how I impact your lives through my actions and words.

I did have a little bit of a struggle with the hair loss initially (Who am I kidding? It's still a bit of struggle today.) BUT health is more important than vanity.

And in the words of Jason, "Your hair will grow back. You're doing chemotherapy so that the cancer doesn't." This doesn't mean that I will be skipping out on reconstruction though. There is a reason God gave some people skills in plastic surgery.

Finally, ladies, here is your reminder to please perform your monthly breast self-exam. If any of you ever find something in your breasts that you think is suspicious, my recommendation is to get it checked as soon as possible and urge your doctor to order a mammogram. I also strongly encourage you to have your baseline mammogram by the age of 35.

Remember "Early detection, Early cure." Life, health, family, friends and faith are precious. Don't ignore what your body is telling you out of fear. Be strong.

Love and peace to you all,
Sharyl

Tests, Tests and More Tests

Wednesday, November 12, 2008

The Saver family has had quite a few weeks. I had a routine ovarian cancer screening blood test on October 16th and four days later the doctor's office called me to tell me the blood test showed elevated numbers.

My doctor ordered a PET/CT scan to see if there was anything going on in my abdomen area. She was concerned mainly with ovarian cancer. I did the scan on October 24th and the results came back with some areas of concern in my lymph nodes—not my ovaries, which excludes ovarian cancer. The only way to see if the areas of concern are cancer is to get a tissue sample.

Herein lies the pickle...

On October 31st, I was sent for an ultrasound-guided biopsy of the area by my collarbone. Neither the ultrasound tech nor the radiologist could locate the lymph node of concern. My doctor and I spoke on November 3rd, and she suggested I see a colleague of hers who is a cardiothoracic specialist. He wanted me to have a chest CT first to determine if he could see the area and if he could, he would then do a procedure to get a tissue sample—a rather invasive procedure.

On Monday, I went for the CT and it didn't show enlarged lymph nodes, so the cardiothoracic specialist didn't want to attempt the procedure. Now I'll be going to see a GI specialist on Wednesday who will put a small tube down the back of my throat with an ultrasound probe at the end of a scope to see if they can locate the area of concern and get a tissue sample.

If they can get a tissue sample and biopsy, I should have an answer by the following Tuesday. If they cannot get a sample my doctor is pretty confident that it is not cancer, and I will repeat a PET scan in December.

I should point out that PET scans are very sensitive to glucose, and infections or mild virus can light up under such scans. I did a blood test that can help identify the recurrence of breast cancer (which, by the way, is what they are looking for) on October 29th. Anything under 37 is normal and my number was 16. Two other views (ultrasound and CT) did not show any enlarged areas.

And, most importantly, the risk of breast cancer recurrence for me is 10%. I have no breast tissue. I had no lymph node involvement in my initial cancer. And, I did eight treatments of very intense chemotherapy drugs that would have killed any stray cancer cells in my body.

Our instincts tell us that I am, as we have believed for over a year now, a very healthy 38-year-old woman. I am sharing this information with all of you because I know that you have prayed, loved and supported me, either for all of my life or since our lives connected.

I won't lie and say that I'm not nervous for the test next week. I am, mainly because it just kind of freaks me out having a scope put down the back of my throat. But, as you all know, I firmly believe in prayer and the more prayer the better. There is strength in numbers!

I am so blessed to have you all in my life, and I appreciate and feel your loving thoughts and prayers. I will let you know as soon as I hear something.

Love,
Sharyl

"Oh, I Remember, I'm Radioactive."
—Steve Martin

Thursday, November 20, 2008

I don't remember the test, so if it was uncomfortable I really don't know. I fell asleep from a combination of a Benadryl and Versed. I was even going to argue with the nurse that they really didn't do the test because I only shut my eyes for a minute. It's just like when I lay my head on the couch at the cabin. I only shut my eyes for a minute but wake up and it's already morning.

Anyway, from what I remember from my conversation with the doctor after the procedure, there was nothing that they could biopsy. He didn't see anything suspicious enough to take a tissue sample, and he could have caused more harm than good by trying to get a sample.

The nurse at my oncologist's office called yesterday afternoon to say my doctor thinks it's great news, so I will repeat the PET/CT scan and ovarian tumor marker (CA-125) and breast tumor marker (CA 27-29) blood tests on December 10th. She will then compare the two PET scans, and if the lymph nodes don't light up again, then all is well.

And with a third injection of radioactive dye in one month, I can use Steve Martin's line, "Oh, I remember, I'm radioactive," and probably really mean it. I do get a kick out of the fact that they tell you it's not harmful, but the person who injects the dye stands behind a metal screen for protection. Hmmm.

Because of my family history of breast cancer, my oncologist will probably always tend to be a little overly cautious with test results that in people who haven't had cancer would otherwise seem insignificant. What I can learn from the last month is that I need to remain calm if for some reason in the future, the doctor would like me to do a test because another test came back a little funky. This is science after all and prone to errors and misreadings.

Thanks to you all for keeping me in your thoughts and prayers. I feel a little selfish asking for prayers, but I tell you what, I felt so much relief within an hour of my request. I truly felt your love and prayers. (Jason thanks you also—I wasn't quite the raging emotional lunatic anymore!!)

I wish you all a very, very Happy Thanksgiving. I am grateful and thankful for each one of you. And, I pray that God blesses each one of your lives and families with the desires of your hearts.

With loving thoughts,
Sharyl

p.s. If I talked to you yesterday, I apologize. I was very, very sleepy and not much in the mood for conversation.

Please Excuse My Moodiness

Wednesday, December 17, 2008

In case you were wondering, I mentioned I was having follow up tests in December, and I had another PET scan last Wednesday. I also had the ovarian tumor marker (CA-125) and breast tumor marker (CA 27-29) blood tests. The blood tests can be helpful in indentifying a recurrence of cancer.

The CA 27-29 (breast) test normal is under 37. I am still at 16, so that's good. The CA 125 (ovarian) test normal is under 35, I was at 180 on October 16th and 148 on December 10th. It has come down, but not enough to be in the normal range. Neither my oncologist nor my gynecological oncologist knows why the number is elevated but they agree that I should have my ovaries and fallopian tubes removed as soon as possible.

So, on January 6th, I will have a little bit more of my female anatomy removed. Please excuse my moodiness while I adjust to menopause at the ripe old age of 38.

The PET scan showed the same spots lighting up, however all but three of the spots are either smaller or lighter on the scan. So, that's good. My doctor said she would be very surprised if this turned out to be or turned into cancer. She indicated that the more tests you have, the more you open yourself up to false positives. She will repeat another PET scan in late February or early March just to monitor the areas that were lighting up.

Happy, Happy Christmas and much love to you all. I pray that you and your families are abundantly blessed with your hopes, dreams and desires for the New Year.

Love,
Sharyl

Turning Uncertainty into a Positive

Friday, March 6, 2009

I had a repeat PET on February 29th. The nurse called me Monday to tell me that the areas in my lymph nodes were gone. Yay! BUT, there was a new spot on my liver. :-(

So, my doctor wanted me to get an MRI. I've never had the pleasure of having an MRI before, and I have to say it was one of the most obnoxious medical tests that I've had so far. It involves being inserted into a metal tube with headphones to drown out the "tapping" that occurs while you're inside the machine. Tapping my butt—I thought I was in a war zone for crying out loud. Between the "tapping" and the bombs and sirens going off, I guess I could at least take comfort in knowing I was safe from the gunfire in the bomb shelter.

The worst part of the test was the blood draw. I can only have blood draws, IVs and blood pressure taken from my left arm due to the lymph nodes removed on my right side. My poor left arm has been beaten to heck over the last two years. After eight rounds of chemo, five surgeries and numerous injections and blood draws, my veins are wise to needles and can be very stubborn.

After five unsuccessful attempts, the tech said, "I hate to go in your hand because the veins are smaller and can hurt more." I told him that I've had chemo drugs running through my hand for four hours, and I thought I could handle 40 minutes in the metal tube. So, the hand it was.

Well, I went to my doctor yesterday and she said they were able to see the spot on my liver on the MRI as well, and she wants me to have a CT-guided liver biopsy next Wednesday. She doesn't believe this is cancer but cannot in good conscience leave it alone and repeat a scan in three months and be responsible for ignoring it if it turns out to be cancer.

I'm still only seven weeks out from my ovarian removal surgery and, as a result, am now in menopause, which can leave fatty deposits on your liver. However, fatty deposits wouldn't light up under a pet scan unless inflamed. Since the liver processes everything, I asked about the four injections of radioactive dye from the scans floating around in my body. She said too much of the dye is not a good thing and also said the anesthetics from the surgery could still be processing.

The radiologist who read the report is convinced it is a metastatic spot, which would mean the breast cancer has developed in my liver. But he also said the cancer in my lymph nodes responded to the treatment I was undergoing. Now if by treatment he means red wine, well then I guess that worked. My doctor said this is why she sometimes doesn't do these scans for her patients because they have a 17-20% false positive rate, which turns into more testing and more follow-ups. It can be an exercise in chasing your tail.

Once again, I'm a little on edge about the uncertainty of it all. My husband and I were in the same room with the doctor, and it's funny how I took the uncertainty and turned it into a negative and Jason digested the same information and all he heard was the positive. This morning I came to the realization that I need to learn from my husband. Jason would see a glass of water that some people would see as half empty and others would see as half full, and he would pour the water into a smaller glass and say "My cup runneth over."

I should have results back by the end of next week. Have a great weekend. We have a weekend free from hockey. What will we do with our free time?

Love,
Sharyl

My Liver is a Little Sore Today

Thursday, March 12, 2009

The liver biopsy went okay, I guess. They are not sure that they got enough of a sample even though they took nine tissue samples from my liver. They sedated me for the test but not enough to knock me out because you do have to participate a little. However, they did give me enough that I didn't care that they were taking little tiny samples of my liver. They told me that I could end up having to do an ultrasound-guided biopsy. Sometimes they can see better with one machine versus another. Whatever.

My liver is a little sore today. Weird thing to say, I know. I probably won't get the results or know if I have to do yet another test until Monday. I do have to say that the lady who put my IV in yesterday was one of the best IV putter-inners ever! Successful on the first attempt and no pain or bruising.

I told a few of you already but I did get blood tests back on Friday for the CA-125 (ovarian) and CA27-29 (breast) tumor markers. The ovarian number is down to 96; still above the normal range (35), but continuing to drop. December's number was 148 and October's 180. The breast marker is still holding at 16, well below the normal range of 37. Both of those numbers are encouraging.

I pray that I will be able to share good news with you all next week. Thanks for your encouraging thoughts, words and prayers. Have a great day and weekend.

With much love,
Sharyl

Pins and Needles

Tuesday, May 19, 2009

Well, I'm on them again—pins and needles that is. A PET scan last Tuesday showed that the lymph nodes under my left arm (opposite arm of original tumor) are lighting up and the spot on my liver still lights up and is now larger.

I had an armpit lymph node biopsy yesterday and am awaiting the results. And, I have a repeat liver biopsy tomorrow—this time guided by ultrasound versus CT.

In addition, my ovarian-tumor marker is elevated again to 177. (It was 96 in February.) My breast-tumor marker is at 24, which is still in the normal range but eight points higher than in February.

I pray for good news from the lymph-node biopsy and the liver biopsy. I'm having a hard time with the waiting and could use some prayer covering from my family and friends. I hope that I am just the girl who cried wolf!

With loving and hopeful thoughts,
Sharyl

Fight Like a Girl

Believe and Pray with Me

Tuesday, May 26, 2009

As most of you may have heard (and for those of you who haven't, I'm sorry to throw it on you like this), I found out last week that I have a recurrence of the breast cancer that invaded my body two years ago. I have a spot on my liver, which is cancerous and a few lymph nodes under my left arm which are cancerous as well. I saw my doctor today, and I will be starting chemotherapy on Friday.

The chemotherapy treatment is part of a clinical trial sponsored by the Mayo Clinic for people who've had a recurrence of triple-negative breast cancer, like me. In the breast cancer world, they diagnose the tumors to see if they are positive or negative for estrogen, progesterone and HER2/neu and this determines what types of chemotherapy and drugs can be used to treat the cancer cells. With triple-negative breast cancer, the cancer cells don't respond to standard hormone-based treatments.

I will be on a three-week cycle of treatment for the next six months, with two weeks on and one week off. My doctor feels this is a slow-growing cancer but likely started developing back in October with the elevation of a CA125 blood test, which prompted the removal of my ovaries.

Unfortunately, some stray cancer cells must have been released in my blood stream during the development of the original cancer, and even though we did everything we could have and should have done at the time to prevent cancer from recurring, these wretched cells have minds of their own.

I know all of this sounds grim and scary, but I believe I will be healed. I have faith that this treatment will zap out the cancerous cells and put me into remission for a very long time. (Like 40 years or so.) I ask that you believe and pray with me. Right now, that is the most important thing you can do for me, along with your positive energy, encouragement and loving support. My family and I are so very blessed to be surrounded by such love and friendship.

Love,
Sharyl

†

Shar,
You are my ROCK! You will overcome this obstacle just as you have many others before. Your faith, love for your family and passion for life can overcome any hurdle that comes your way. I Love You and look forward to the day the doctor says the cancer is gone, once and for all!

Love,
Di

†

Sharyl,
We love you and are praying and believing with you!!!

Loréal and Aaron

Freedom and Deliverance from Cancer!

Sunday, May 31, 2009

Yesterday, I was filled with so much energy! I'm not sure if it was a little of the steroid from the anti-nausea medication still in me, but I will take it.

I started cleaning my house and when I clean, I always enjoy a little music to help me along. So I put in one of my favorite cleaning artists, Dolly Parton. In my opinion, she is one of the best female artists of our time. As I was singing and cleaning, one of my favorite Dolly songs came on, a song she released back in the mid to late 70's about freedom and deliverance, and that is exactly what I am claiming from cancer!

As the words of "Light of a Clear Blue Morning" were flowing from Dolly through my mouth, I was declaring that by the light of the clear blue morning, everything's gonna be alright, it's gonna be okay. As I danced and sang in the kitchen, Jacob came in to say, "Mom, you woke me up," and I replied, "That's okay because everything is gonna be alright! It's gonna be okay!"

Yesterday, I cleaned, danced, visited Jason at the fire station, went to Sam's Club, got gas, folded clothes and took my dog for a walk—all before 2:30 p.m. So much of everything in life is attitude, which made me think of the Sleepy Eye, Minn., teen who was ordered to start chemo last Thursday.

The 10 p.m. news on Friday reported he was angry because he was sick from chemo. I was saddened to think this young boy is so angry and that some of his support system is also angry. I respect him and his family in their disagreement with the treatment, but I pray they will change their mindsets and rid themselves of their anger and negativity.

Many of you have offered to help our family with watching our kids, and we will need help for doctor visits and things like that, but keep in mind that I intend for the most part to feel very good throughout my treatment. I don't like to be alone, so if you are going to invite my kids somewhere, please ask if I would like to come along or stop by and visit.

I want to talk about your kids, your family, your joys, celebrations and things that may be troubling you. I want to tell you about my kids, their activities, the trip my husband is planning for us to Colorado to celebrate our 10-year anniversary and basically to remember that there is so much more to life than cancer!

Have a great day, enjoy the weather, and post, email or call anytime.

Love,
Sharyl

†

Hey CHERRY!
You have so many people pulling for you. If prayers and good thoughts alone could cure you, your friends and family would have you healed a thousand times over by now!

Love,
Brenda

†

"I feel blessed that I still have the little Dolly in my heart. I'm still the same girl that wants to squeeze every little drop out of life that I can."—Dolly Parton

Nicky

Pesky Little Bugger

Tuesday, June 2, 2009

I've been thinking about this recurrence thing, and I spent the better part of the week of May 22nd really beating myself up. It just didn't make sense. I exercise four to five days a week, with a combination of running, weight training and plyometric aerobics. I eat relatively clean, with the exception of red meat and chips. Oh, and overindulgence of red wine or beer on occasion.

My morning smoothie consists of flax seed, which is supposed to help keep breast cancer away. I take calcium with vitamin D daily because I knew I was going to have my ovaries removed, and I needed to have a strong bone base when they ripped the last bit of estrogen from my body, which also can lower risk of breast cancer.

So truly, what did I do to make it come back??? What I realized is, unfortunately, triple-negative breast cancer can be a pesky little bugger. But one of the positive things my doctor said to me was that this was a slow-growing cancer. And, I believe that is due to all of things I am doing above. My body feels great, and I feel strong and healthy. I was out for short jog yesterday—two-and-a-half miles at a slower pace than normal and no hills, except the small one near our house. I hope to get another short jog in today and tomorrow.

I plan on changing the face of cancer and the way one looks and acts during treatment. I will continue to exercise as much as I can throughout my treatment, whether through the activities above or less-intensive activities like low-impact aerobics and walking. I have shared many times with my family and friends that exercise is a hobby of mine and something that I can control. It is empowering for me!

I don't know what the future holds except that **I will** have a long future with my family and friends. My friend Brenda is right. The prayers and positive thoughts you all have covered me in could have cured me 1,000 times over. Nicky, thanks for sharing the "Dollyism." We should all try to squeeze every little drop out of life that we can.

Keep your guestbook entries coming. They fuel my strength, faith and hope so that I can put this cancer thing behind me once and for all.

Love,
Sharyl

†

Shar Bear,
You have many years of singing and dancing ahead of you. I Love You and will see you through every step of this journey, and we will look back at this time on our kids' wedding days and revel in the fact that you conquered this ugly disease.

I Love You!
Di

Slow Down and Enjoy Life

Thursday, June 4, 2009

Today, we went with Taylor to visit the University of Wisconsin at River Falls, and it went very well. I'm so excited for him to make this transition to complete his education. I know he will do wonderfully. It is bittersweet to be at this point in your child's life. He is a great kid, and we are so very proud of his accomplishments. He will be an amazing teacher or rock star someday, or perhaps both!

Tomorrow, I have the second treatment in my first round of chemo. I hope I will feel as well after this treatment as I did after last week's treatment. I will keep you all posted.

I learned something this week while out jogging. It's kind of a cliché, but sometimes it just takes a different situation to make it sink in. I don't claim to be a marathoner or in the process of training for one, but in the past when I'd run it was all about competing with myself. To add another hill, shave off more time, or go longer.

I started taking my dog Blazer running with me a few months ago. I felt bad every time I left him at home so that I could do hill runs or go longer because I was told he would wait by the door while I was gone. So, I made a point of taking him with me every time I went. This became a very big source of frustration for me while running because I couldn't go as long as I wanted, I couldn't go as fast as I wanted, and I certainly couldn't take him up hills.

I would spend the run tugging at Blazer to make him go faster. And although he kept a pretty good pace, when I got home, I would feel like it was a wasted run. The running was becoming a letdown because I was not "bettering" myself.

This week, when I decided I should jog rather than run so as not to deplete all my energy, I found that after the jog I felt fantastic. I was not stripped of all my energy, Blazer and I bonded, and we ran as a team. I was not tugging at him to make him go faster, I enjoyed my surroundings more, and I was so much more aware of my body and what it could do. My head felt so much clearer after these jogs than my "I have to run a few seconds faster than I did yesterday" runs.

So, I guess the moral of my story is slow down and life becomes much more enjoyable!

Love,
Sharyl

†

Sharyl,
You have been through more challenges so far in your life than almost anyone I know. Every time, you have done an unbelievable job of not only surviving the situation, but also making something positive out of it and becoming a stronger woman.

After your first cancer diagnosis and treatment, you emerged as a healthy, beautiful woman inside and out. Every time I have run into you over the past two years, you have been smiling and upbeat. I know that your positive attitude, fighting spirit, faith, family and friends will get you through this latest challenge.

I will continue to think and pray for you daily.

God bless,
Jenelle

Letter from Taylor

Thursday, June 4, 2009

Mom,

You are my hero. I want you to know that. Your enduring spirit, faith and attitude are something that **everyone** can learn from. It amazes me that while going through chemotherapy you still have the will, strength and determination to run darn near every day while also, I may add, going to work every day and being a full-time mother. But knowing you, I would expect nothing other.

There was a time when you were the only parent I had to look up to, and I must say that there is no better example of a hard-working, dedicated parent. That alone is worthy of hero status in my eyes. But then, from being a single mother working her way through college, motherhood and life in general to a happily married woman dealing with the loss of a child and then facing the diagnosis of an evil damn disease...twice.

Never once have I seen you stumble, lose your faith or back down from the fight against what life can throw at you. With all that you have been through—all we have been through—never have you faltered in your steadfast strength and will. That is why you are my hero. I believe that your faith in and love of God has much to do with this, for never have I seen you question the power of faith. I believe that the faith of others in you and your faith in yourself is worth more than any words spoken from a doctor's mouth.

You are my hero. **You are a hero to all of us**. Don't stress over the "how," for God—at least my God—doesn't "test" people in this way, by giving people "what they can handle." It was no more his will than it was anything you have done, for our genetics are out of our control. He doesn't work in that way; I don't care what anyone says. God didn't get you into this, but I believe faith can get you out. And you have no shortage of that. No shortage of faith in yourself or of others in you.

Seeing the heartfelt hellos, promises of prayers and just plain kind words shared by so many of our friends, family and some distant acquaintances is proof enough that there are many people here for you, all with faith in you. You are not alone.

Mom, I love you with all my heart, and I owe you a whole heck of a lot for all you have done for me and for our family. I can honestly say I wouldn't be the young man I am today without you as a role model for how to act as an adult, how to react in the face of such events and just plainly how to live.

With love, from your oldest and tallest, but always your little boy,
"T" Taylor

†

Sharyl,
I loved reading those heartfelt words from Taylor. What an awesome tribute to you. He obviously has learned so much from your wonderful guidance and the respect and love is very apparent. We are praying for you.

Time to beat this!

Claire

Thanks, Loréal

Friday, June 5, 2009

One of the drugs I'm on lowers white-cell counts and although I feel fantastic, my white counts were on the low side. I was still able to do chemo, but because I'm on the trial they have strict guidelines on the numbers. (If your white counts get too low, it makes it hard for the body to fight infections.)

Since I've already had chemo in the past, it takes my body longer to rebuild between chemo drips than before. Plus, I was getting help last time with a white-cell booster injection, but as part of the clinical trial, the shot is not an option for me. I pray that between now and June 19th my body is able to build back quickly.

My dear, sweet, cousin Loréal from New York works at a very cool restaurant called Michael's. The other day, she was talking to Evelyn Lauder, a VP at Estée Lauder, founder of the Breast Cancer Research Foundation (BCRF) and creator of the pink-ribbon campaign for breast cancer awareness.

Loréal talked with Evelyn about my situation and asked if there are any new treatments on the horizon for triple-negative breast cancer. Evelyn gave Loréal the name of woman at the foundation, and Loréal emailed her and learned about a doctor at the Mayo Clinic. Within a couple of hours, my cousin had received an email back from the woman at BCRF that the doctor at Mayo had responded to her and would be more than happy to set up a phone conversation.

I called his office today, and it was already noted that I would be calling. The doctor was busy but called me back about 30 minutes later and said if I could gather all of my info, he could see me Tuesday. He said that there is a lot of research being done right now on triple-negative breast cancer.

My sister Dianna, the kids and I are going up to our cabin in a little while to relax for the weekend. Have a happy weekend!

Love,
Sharyl

†

Hey Shar,
Have we told you lately how strong and beautiful you are—inside and out? Cancer has met its match, and you will win! Never forget that you have an entire army of people right behind you who will do anything to help you beat this thing.

Love you lots,
Michael, Kristin, Emma and Luke

†

Sharyl and family,
We are all praying for you. We are blessed to have such a strong beautiful woman like you in our lives! Keep fighting to beat this! We are all here to support you in this mission!

Love you,
Jamie and Hunter

Turning the Negative into Positive

"Impossible is an opinion, not a fact."
—Muhammad Ali

Monday, June 8, 2009

I had a very nice and relaxing weekend with Di and our kids at the cabin, where we just hung out and had a relaxing time. We watched movies and TV, read and, of course, ate! I feel very good!

I spent this afternoon after work stopping at three clinics to pick up scans, slides and CDs of my body to take with me to Mayo tomorrow.

A group of my friends brought me some books to pass the time during chemo, waiting rooms and car rides. I'm reading, *Crazy Sexy Cancer Tips* by Kris Carr. Kris and I seem to have very similar attitudes and views. She has a completely different type of canser, but the book offers wonderful tips and ways to look at things, some of which I am already doing. One thing she mentioned, which I've been trying not to do is to refer to the canser that recurred in my body as "my" canser.

I refuse to refer to canser as a possession of mine. I really don't want it and will do whatever it takes to make it go away. Another tip she gave was to even go so far as to misspell it. I love this idea! As someone with an uncommon spelling of her name, it can be a tich annoying when it is misspelled. Most people don't misspell names intentionally, but I'm going to be a brat and purposely misspell canser.

Another wonderful story from the book is when a perfectly placed billboard was put in her path. (It probably helped that David Beckham was on the billboard.) It quoted Muhammad Ali:

"Impossible is just a big word thrown around by small men who find it easier to live in the world they've been given than to explore the power they have to change it.

Impossible is an opinion, not a fact. Impossible isn't a declaration, it's a dare. Impossible is potential. Impossible is temporary. Impossible is nothing."

What Kris did when she saw this billboard was to replace the word "impossible" with "incurable." Since at this moment in time there is no medical cure for canser, I love the idea of taking the negativity of the word "incurable" and making it a very real and close possibility.

I hope you all had a great day. I'm looking forward to my visit at Mayo tomorrow and finding out more about the hope for a cure!

Love,
Sharyl

†

Hello friend!
I've seen you overcome struggles in your life, and I praise you for the great strength and courage you have shown throughout.

I know that you will continue to do what you do best, which is to never give up as you fight to get cured. You are the strong, beautiful, optimistic and loving Sharyl! I LOVE YOU DEARLY, and if you need anything you know where to find me. Can't wait to hear how Mayo went!

Steph

Laughing Across Life's Bumpy Roads

Tuesday, June 9, 2009

My trip to the Mayo Clinic went very well. I met with a very nice doctor. He said I look great and was very happy I'm tolerating chemo well. He said that can have a lot to do with the success of the treatment—that and faith and a positive attitude. I'm happy to know that had he seen me three weeks ago, he would have recommended the same chemotherapy treatment I'm on. The local clinic I'm going to is in the research network with Mayo, and I plan on continuing my chemotherapy there.

The doctor said the trends and emphasis on research change and right now there is a big emphasis on triple-negative breast canser research. Five years ago, there was an emphasis on HER2/neu-positive research, and they have had a lot of success with the resulting treatment options and long-term survival rates.

I got the feeling this doctor felt that with the emphasis on the treatment of triple-negative breast canser they will see the long-term survival rates for triple-negative cansers increasing as well.

So many of you mention about my being positive and staying positive. I have a little help in that department. I'm a firm believer that laughter is great medicine, and I'm so blessed to have a spouse who makes me laugh. When I first introduced Jason to my friends, they would say, "He's so funny; you must laugh all the time." I would roll my eyes and say, "He's really not that funny."

But the truth is that he really is funny, and we do laugh a lot together. Sometimes he "forces" me to smile and laugh. And, he always insists on taking these pictures of us that at times I find annoying. But then looking back on the pictures, it takes me back to that moment and although sometimes I think it was a really sad time, at the same time I remember that my husband asked me to smile in an effort to say "I promise we will get through this," and each time we have.

I've included a picture from chemo last Friday that he made me take with him. At first I was annoyed, because do I really want a picture of us while crazy chemicals are running through my veins? And the answer is "Yes," so that someday we can look back and say, "See, we made it through another one of life's bumps in the road!"

I pray that each one of you has someone or something in your life that makes you smile and laugh!

Love,
Sharyl

†

Sharyl,

I am so happy that your meeting at Mayo went well and that the doctor agrees with your course of treatment. You are a very strong woman with an immense amount of love around you, and I pray God will continue to pour more and more of His strength and love into you so that others are lifted up by it. Your posts encourage and inspire me. I love you!

Loréal

Smile and Laugh Often. It Feels Good!

Monday, June 15, 2009

I hope you all had a great weekend. I'm feeling very good. I talked to my doctor this morning because I wasn't sure I wanted to continue in the trial since my white-cell counts are low. The last two Fridays, I've left the clinic feeling like the sky was falling.

This morning, my doctor reassured me that although my white cells are low, they are not low enough to cause the kind of concern some of the staff indicated this past Friday.

I have an appointment with her on Thursday and will have another blood test that day. She felt my numbers would rebound enough by then to have chemo on Friday, and if they are not high enough, they can adjust the dosage of the drug. She said the amount they gave me on the first two treatments of each drug were the full doses they would give people who were just receiving one of the drugs.

I feel much better after speaking with her and understanding a little bit more about the study guidelines and modifications. I have chemo this Friday and the following Friday, and then I will have scans to measure the success of my healing!

I hope you all have a happy day. Smile and laugh often. It feels good!

Love,
Sharyl

†

Sharyl,

It was sooo hard to get your news when your Dad and I were so far away, but I am encouraged by your strength and faith that you will get past this. You are a beautiful, strong woman, and we are so proud of the things you have done. You have been and are a wonderful daughter, wife, mother, sister and friend.

Laughter has always been your gift, and I know that will help you through these times. I remember being told by your teachers that you laughed too much, but I always felt it was your ability to laugh that made you so pleasant to be with. So keep laughing, remain strong in your faith and remember God has plans for you.

Keep your positive attitude, and remember always that I love you,
Mom

Take My Hand. I'll Be There.

Wednesday, June 17, 2009

My mom sent a couple of pictures of me as a little girl that she thought I should share. She captioned the first one "Laughter is the best medicine" because I have quite the smile and laugh during this family photo. I'm sure my brother Michael was doing something silly to make me laugh. I have been told my laugh is contagious, so why not share it.

The second picture is kind of hard to see, but it is of my sister Dianna and me at a local festival called Kaposia Days back in 1976. We used to go to the high school and participate in their family activities and then watch the fireworks. They had races for the kids, and my sister and I were a little nervous so we came up with the idea that it would be best to run the race holding hands.

My mom titled this picture "Take my hand, I'll be there," which is exactly what my little sis has done for me in so many ways over the years. I have this picture in my bedroom, and I've looked at it many times. It is very hard to determine who is who, but I think I'm the chubby-faced one trailing behind.

I'm feeling good. I've had a few headaches at night, which have been disrupting my sleep, but we've had a busy week with Abby's dance rehearsal and recital, so I think that may have something to do with it. Tonight is the first night of her show. She makes a very cute and convincing firefighter, ghostbuster and cheerleader.

Have a super day. Smile and laugh often,
Sharyl

†

Sharyl and family,

I was at church the day I heard of the canser return. I started to cry—tears slowly coming during the rest of the service—thinking of you and your family.

But after reading your entries, crying doesn't seem at all the deal. Instead, I see an amazing woman who will be lifting others up in their struggles for a long time to come. Thank YOU for sharing your journey with us.

You Go, Girl!
Robin

†

To My Favorite Sister-in-Law,
Your strength amazes me, Sharyl. You are an inspiration and are very loved by many!

Love,
Danielle

Praise God. Hip Hip Hooray!

Thursday, June 18, 2009

First, I just want to say Happy 20th Birthday to Taylor, my oldest, tallest, but always my little boy. We wish you a year filled with love, laughter and abundant blessings. You are a wonderful young man. I love you!

Second, thanks to all of you for your prayers, faith and positive thoughts. Praise God, my white counts were great. Last Friday, my neutrophils were 900. In order to receive chemo tomorrow at the full dose they needed to be at 1,500, which is the the low side of normal. My neutrophils are 2,100, the middle of the normal range.

Prior to chemo, my doctor was able to feel the enlarged lymph nodes under my arm. She cannot feel them now. Again, I say Praise God. Hip Hip Hooray! (I will always be a cheerleader at heart.)

I'm right on track for my treatment. After next Friday, the study guidelines are less rigid and modifications can be made.

Thanks so much for your guestbook entries. They fill me with tremendous encouragement. Thank you too for the meals that have been coming our way. Jacob hesitantly tells me the dinners are very good while assuring me that my cooking is good too.

Love,
Sharyl

True Companion

Friday, June 19, 2009

Abby has her final night of recital tonight. Throughout this week, I have been watching her dance along with my two nieces at rehearsal and the dance recital, and it reminded me how much I love dance. Dancing fills me with so much joy, whether it is watching or participating. Last night, as I watched the boys and girls dance, I couldn't have wiped the smile off my face if I tried.

Ten years ago, a handsome red-haired man and I took a chance when he asked me to take his hand and share a dance. The night of our wedding, we danced to the song "True Companion" by Marc Cohn, and we have been enjoying this dance for the last 10 years. Like a waltz, we have had our ups and downs, but it has been beautiful to watch and be a part of.

I look forward to 40 years from now, when we are surrounded by our children and grandchildren, family and friends celebrating our 50th wedding anniversary. Maybe by then I can even convince Jason to take dance lessons with me so we can masterfully waltz to the song "True Companion."

I love you with all my heart, Jason Allen. You are my hero. Here's to 10 great years. I am excited to see what the next 40 years bring us!

God bless,
Sharyl

Fight Like a Girl

Saturday, June 20, 2009

Today, Jason and I spent the day in Minneapolis. We stopped by the Twins Autograph party, but they were sold out of the cards so we just bummed around town. We went to lunch and then walked down to the river, across the bridge and back to the Metrodome to watch the Twins blow a lead in the 7th inning and, unfortunately, lose the game.

The day after my first chemo treatment, I heard a song on the radio. I didn't pay much attention to it until the last verse when I heard the word "canser." I heard it again one day in my car and then this morning, I thought "I should turn on the radio because I think that song is going to be on," and I turned the radio on just as it started to play.

I thought the song was called "Hold My Head High" but it turns out it's called "Fight Like a Girl," which is even better. This song by Bombshel speaks to me because it's about a young mother with three children whose canser has spread. The song talks about not letting canser define you, standing strong and holding your head high in the face of it. It does refer to canser being a test from God though, and we should all know God does not test us with suffering. But the rest of the song defines my attitude toward this bump in the road.

It's amazing how music can come to you at just the right time to lift you up, fill you with encouragement or comfort your soul.

I hope you are having a great weekend. Happy Father's Day to all of you Dads out there.

To my Dad, I love you. You are a great man. Thank you for always loving me unconditionally. To Jason, thank you for being the light that keeps our family glowing. You are the Father of the Year in our eyes.

Holding my head high and fighting like a girl!
Sharyl

†

Dear Ant Sharyl,
I am thinking about you. My mom took me and Konnor and Baby Carter on a walk tonight. We walked over to the big, huge sand "mountain." We put down our bikes and climbed to the top. Mom even pushed Carts up in the stroller.

I was very excited, because I knew on the mountain that I was even closer to Jesus. (My mom says He is in the sky watching over us.) And I knew if I prayed on the mountain, He for sure would hear my prayers. That is what we all did, and then we played.

Love you. XOXOXOXO
Tanner (and Konnor too, but he isn't allowed near the computer) and Carter

Class of '88—Best Hair

Sunday, June 21, 2009

When I was a senior in high school, we had this section in our yearbook where we would vote on classmates for things like "best athlete," "best eyes," "best walk," etc.

I was voted "best hair." I graduated in 1988 and back in '88, as many of you will remember, "hair bands" ruled the air and video waves. It was all about hair, so all of us girls had great hair.

When I was a freshman in high school, I got a short haircut and hated it. From that haircut on, I decided I was going to have long hair for a long time. Over the years, I tried a few times to cut my hair short but would always go back to long hair. When I was first diagnosed with breast canser in 2007 and was informed that I would have to undergo chemotherapy, the first thought that came to mind was, "I don't want to lose my hair." It had become my identity, my security blanket. What would I do without it???

Next to me, I think my son Jacob had the hardest time with my hair loss. But we all got used to my bald head around the house, and I spent that summer sporting either a wig or a hat. I finished chemo in September '07, and my hair started growing back in late November. I finally felt comfortable enough to take off my security blanket in March '08. It was very hard for me at first to go out in public with my super short hair, but I overcame my fear and even began to like the new, crazy, curly hair growing out of my head. Curly hair was foreign to me since I have always had stick-straight hair. (It took a power curling iron and lots of hair spray to pull off that look in the late 80's and early 90's.)

Over the last few months, I had grown to love the short hair I was sporting. In fact, a few days before my recurrence diagnosis, I had an appointment to cut my hair because it was getting too long. I was trying to figure out how I was going to tell Jacob that I may not grow my hair long anymore.

I hoped when the side effect listing for the new chemo drug said "hair thinning" that my hair would just thin a little. And, while I could stand to thin out my now very thick head of hair, over the course of this last week, every morning I have combed out more and more until now all that is left are some straggly hairs. But, my doctor told me that unlike the last chemo drugs that stop hair from growing until you are done with chemo, with the drugs I'm on now, the hair will start to grow back while I'm still receiving them.

Losing my hair this time is not nearly as traumatic as it was the first time, but it still sucks! I'm human. I like to look good and a nice head of hair on a woman sure helps to enhance our overall looks. But, I will just throw on my wig for work and when I'm out and about and want to look more like myself. I will have to go hat shopping again for the hot days, when a wig is too much. And, who knows, maybe this time my hair will grow back straight.

God bless. Have a great week. Laugh and smile often.

Holding my head high and fighting like a girl,
Sharyl

Confessions of a Canser Runner

I Hope You Dance

Wednesday, June 24, 2009

I've mentioned how much I love to dance. It has always been a part of my life. I started taking dance when I was a young girl and took lessons up until I graduated from high school.

In my 20's, dancing became something fun to do with friends. I remember many a Thursday night spent at Grandma's Saloon in Minneapolis where my friend Steph and I whipped our long, blond manes around the dance floor.

I was so excited last summer when I was dancing to my brother's band, the Lid Twisters, at a bar by our cabin called the Cabaret, and my hair was long enough to simulate hair whipping. I woke up the next morning with a very sore neck from all the dancing we did that night. I blame it on that darn "Cowboy Boots" song—it gets me every time.

A few years ago, I took adult dance classes offered by my former teacher, who is now Abby's dance teacher. Julie is quite a beautiful dancer, and it is a true joy to watch her tap those feet and still be able to kick her nose when she dances. Anyway, I took this class from her, and it was so much fun. I even performed in the end-of-the-year review.

There was something very exciting about putting tap and jazz shoes on again to learn dances and perform in a recital. Before I went on stage, I was nervous and self conscious, wondering what people would think of me for doing such a thing. I am not a kid anymore. What was I trying to prove? But it was an amazing experience, and I'm going to sign up for her summer adult classes as another part of my healing process. I also hope to take classes from her next year and participate in her 30th Dance Review. After all, I performed in her first dance review.

Through dance, we celebrate many rites of passage, such as proms, father-daughter dances, and weddings. I'm sure many of you have heard the Lee Ann Womack song "I Hope You Dance." The first time I heard it was a few months after our daughter Caylin passed away from a skin disorder called epidermolysis bullosa at six weeks of age. The music video features Lee Ann with her daughters. Her youngest was about one-year old at the time, and, in my mind, she bore a striking resemblance to Caylin.

The video shows Lee Ann watching her girls dance, and her hope for them is to "dance" in life. I think we all have that hope for our children, and I couldn't help but think Caylin was hoping the same for us. That despite our sadness and broken hearts, when faced with the choice to sit it out or dance, she hopes we dance. I plan on dancing and giving faith a fighting chance throughout my life. Hopefully you will join me in doing the same.

Love,
Sharyl

p.s. Speaking of dancing, the Lid Twisters will be performing at a street dance sponsored by the South St. Paul Lions Club for Kaposia Days. Maybe they will perform "Cowboy Boots." Trust me, by the second verse you will think you have known this song your whole life...

p.p.s. These are pictures of my sweet little Abby from the recital representing two of my favorite things: a dancer/cheerleader, and also her daddy as a firefighter.

p.p.p.s. I have chemo on Friday and a CT scan on Monday to measure the shrinking of the canser! (Pray for a good stick. Even though it's their job to stick people all day long, it's amazing how much trouble these people can have...)

†

Sharyl,

These words from Psalm 30:10-13 made me think of you after reading your journal today:

Hear, LORD, and be merciful to me; LORD, be my help. You turned my wailing into dancing; you removed my sackcloth and clothed me with joy, that my heart may sing your praises and not be silent. LORD my God, I will praise you forever.

Your courage and strength are beautiful tributes to your faith. Your love for life is contagious, and I hope you never stop dancing.

Love you,
Mom

PARP Inhibitors Offer Hope

Thursday, June 25, 2009

The Mayo Clinic doctor mentioned that a big emphasis on research for inherited cansers is on PARP Inhibitors, a class of enzyme inhibitors. From what I've read, blocking an enzyme's activity can kill a pathogen or correct a metabolic imbalance.

Canser cells that are low in oxygen—fast-growing tumors like mine—are sensitive to PARP Inhibitors, making them a promising treatment option. The PARP Inhibitor treatment is taken by pill and doesn't have the hair loss and nausea side effects that come with chemotherapy drugs.

The research on PARP Inhibitors has mainly focused on people with the genetic mutations of BRCA1 and BRCA2, which increase your lifetime risk for breast and ovarian canser to 85% and 40%, respectively, and for men can increase the risk of prostate canser.

This morning on the Today show, they had a segment on the success of PARP Inhibitor research. This is great news for someone like me who has a mutated BRCA1 gene. I hope not to need a PARP Inhibitor, because the chemotherapy that I'm doing now will remove canser from my body, and I will be done with this silly canser thing once and for all.

Holding my head high and fighting like a girl,
Sharyl

My Whining for the Day

Monday, June 29, 2009

Chemo went well on Friday. I feel good. I do have a little summer cold that is kind of an annoyance, but not a big deal. I was really hoping to make it out of the scan appointment today without any bruising...

But, unfortunately, three failed attempts tend to leave a mark. I am most disappointed with the nurse who came to "save the day." As if I didn't feel frustrated enough that they had to cut the circulation off in my arm for about 20 minutes before they stabbed me with a needle three times; then, this lady comes with her superior attitude and asks if I've had chemo before.

"Why yes, that is why I am here."

She looks at me very condescendingly and says, "You know ports are wonderful."

I replied, "I realize that, but the Mayo Clinic has guidelines for the clinical trial, and the procedure to insert a port would delay me from being on the trial for six weeks."

This was not acceptable to her, because apparently she is an expert in canser, chemo and clinical trials. She said, "Well, you really might want to think about getting a port in the future." I had to bite my tongue not to respond with a remark. It's not worth it.

I've had four PET scans, which involve IV injections; four treatments of chemo over the last four weeks that involve IV insertions (I realize the needle sizes may be different for each of these things but...); and two liver needle biopsies, which required IVs as well. And all of these people seem to get it on the first try. Maybe it's not just me!

Well, that's my whining for the day. I await great news from my doctor about the scans.

Thanks so much for your prayers, positive thoughts and kind words. Yesterday's gospel at church was about faith and healing.

The homily was so meaningful to me and reinforced everything I believe in: God does not bring us pain, suffering and tragedy but that through faith and grace, He promises that He will stand by our sides and carry us through the tough times.

Holding my head high and fighting like girl,
Sharyl

†

Hello Sharyl!
Here I was on the flight from hell today, complaining about the flight being late, the kids running around the plane and crying, the idiots who have to check their bags at the last minute because they don't fit, the very large woman spilling over into my seat, then spilling her cranberry juice all over me and my things (nice stain!), and the list goes on.

How trivial was I being when you are fighting like a mad woman!?! I need to start being thankful for things like you are. You are so grateful for everything and here I was complaining. I need to take a lesson or two from you. Keep those good results coming!

Brenda

God's Healing Power and Grace

Wednesday, July 1, 2009

Yesterday, I received what we Catholics call the Sacrament of the Anointing of the Sick. It was a very special prayer service/blessing where the priest laid his hands on my head, invoking the healing power of the Holy Spirit, and anointed my forehead and hands. A lovely new friend of mine suggested the service, and I am very grateful she did. Thanks, Beth!

Today, I had my off-week blood test. The last time I talked about the neutrophil numbers (the part of the white cells that help fight infection), my number right before chemo on day one of my second cycle was 2,100, which was right in the middle of the normal range. Today, my number five days after chemo was (drum roll please) 4,000, well into the normal range. My platelets are good, my hemoglobin is great, so all is well. I think my numbers are rebounding due to some nutrition tips my cousin researched for me. Thanks, Julie.

Now for even more exciting news! I asked the nurse if she had a copy of my CT scan results from Monday. She said she would go check. She came back out with very happy eyes and a smile she was trying to hold back.

She said, "After I went back to find them, I thought 'What if it's bad news?'" and then she looked at me and said, "Well, it's not."

The report said the spots on my lymph nodes have regressed, which I believe means they are gone because there were no measurements on the report. And, the liver lesion has decreased in size. Unfortunately, on the copy of the report that I have, the size of the lesion was cut off so I will have to call my doctor to find that out. Most importantly, no new areas have appeared!

This is just the most amazing news, and I say *"Rejoice!"* and again I say, *"Rejoice!"* I am so happy God is healing me and that we are witnessing His healing power and grace.

Thank you all so much for supporting, loving, praying and thinking of me. Your thoughts, words and prayers are what motivate me to keep the faith.

Holding my head high and fighting like a girl! (Sorry but that never gets old for me!)

God bless,
Sharyl

†

Dear Sharyl,
Rejoice in the Lord always: and again I say, Rejoice.
—Philippians 4:4 (KJV)

Love You,
Mom

Happy Birthday to My Hero

Thursday, July 2, 2009

It is my wonderful hubby's birthday today, and I just wanted to wish him a Happy Birthday. He's the hero in my life, so what better picture to share than one of him doing what he loves.

I love you, Jason.
Sharyl

Stay Strong! You Are Not Alone

Wednesday, July 8, 2009

In the book *Crazy Sexy Cancer Tips* by Kris Carr, she gives tips on exercise. She said she learned from Dr. Brian Clement that the **body heals eight times faster with exercise**. I don't know how factual that statistic is, but I have healed quickly from the surgeries I've had. I also have tolerated chemo well, both in 2007 and now. So it stands to reason that the exercising I've been doing over the last 20-some years plays a big part in all of that.

Besides, you never know what kind of support, inspiration and reinforcement you might find while exercising. Over the weekend, I was out jogging with Blazer around the lake at our cabin and passed an older couple walking, and the woman had on an Under Armour "Power in Pink" t-shirt. The couple smiled at me, and the woman and I exchanged glances as if to remind each other to "Stay strong."

I submitted an entry last year for the "Power in Pink: She's a Fighter" survivor campaign, but was not selected. I was going to try again this year, but I got sidetracked with this recurrence thing and forgot to submit my entry. Maybe I will be selected in 2010.

The day before, I was a little self conscious going to the beach with a hat covering my bald head. But when I got there, I saw another woman about my age wearing a bandana on her own bald head. It was another reminder to "Stay strong," and to remember that I'm not alone.

However, you won't see me with a bandana or a scarf around my head (unless there's a hat on top of it). I just can't seem to look like anything other than a very convincing pirate with one of those things on. Add a patch and some earrings, and I could run around yelling "Aaargh," scaring little kids. I guess I don't have the right-shaped head to pull off the scarf look, or I guess I do, depending on how you look at it!

During my jog that morning, I was greeted by many people out walking, jogging and running. But the most inspiring moment was when I passed a 20-something woman jogging, an older woman riding a bike and a young girl about 12 years old, who also was riding a bike and wearing a pink baseball hat to cover her bald head. We all waved, smiled and said hello.

The young girl's smile and sunny disposition motivated me to stay positive and happy. Later in my jog, as a woman about my age came up alongside me and then passed me, I only cared for a moment that she was passing me. I was able to push aside the thought that came to mind, "If I didn't have this summer cold, and if I wasn't going through chemotherapy, there's no way I would let you pass me or have even caught up to me for that matter."

As I turned the corner and let her out of my sight, I was greeted by the two women and the beautiful little girl in the pink baseball hat riding her bike. She reminded me that I am exercising not to compete, but rather because I can and because it feels good.

Laugh and smile often,
Sharyl

p.s. I thought I'd share a picture of me and one of my reasons to keep "Fighting Like a Girl."

Daily Yogurt Does a Body Good

Thursday, July 9, 2009

I love reporting stuff like this. I just got back from the doctor's office; I see her before the start of every chemo cycle. We went over the scan results, and she said it is very good that after only two chemo cycles, the lymph nodes have regressed, meaning the radiologist couldn't see them on the CT scan, and the liver tumor has decreased in size to 1.6 cm from 2.4 cm. Yay!

My doctor finds it very surprising that my white cells are so high. She said if I was not on the study, she would not be giving me the doses of two of the drugs at full strength because of how they wipe out one's white cells. Daily yogurt does a body good.

She then asked me about working, how it's going and if I'm tiring from it. She asked if I feel well enough by Monday to go to work. Not anymore than the average working person, but I have felt well enough to go to work on Saturday if I had to, which I won't because that's dedicated family time!

She finds it hard to believe that I'm feeling so well. I neglected to tell her I had been out for a three-and-a-half mile jog on Friday and Saturday and three-mile jogs on Monday and Tuesday of this week. The medical field can only take so much disbelief in one day! Oh, and one more thing: One of the drugs can raise your blood pressure; Mine is holding steady at 108/64.

Well, it's chemo tomorrow for the third of six cycles. Thank you for the prayer covering. It is felt and appreciated.

Holding my head high, fighting like a girl,
Sharyl

†

Sharyl,

Great news! I guess your doctor just doesn't know who she's dealing with. It's your vibrant, positive, smiling attitude, your strong belief and faith in God, your motivation for self care and your love for life, as well as your willingness to fight like a girl that make you a walking miracle.

Hopefully by the time you finish treatment, you will make a believer out of your doctor as to just what faith, determination and prayer can do. Keep smiling and keep fighting.

Love you,
Mom

†

Sharyl,

It was so nice to see you at Kaposia days. You looked beautiful as always. Doesn't surprise me that you're kicking some cancer butt right now because A) you're a tough cookie and B) you have strong faith in God's incredible healing power. Keep trusting in Him and take comfort in the fact that more people than you know are praying for you daily.

Love,
Liz

Don't Mistake Positivity and Faith for Cockiness

Tuesday, July 14, 2009

When I have chemotherapy, after the nurse gets the IV and the drugs going and the mess cleaned up, she comes back to ask a list of questions with respect to the side effects I have experienced over the last week or two.

Friday, the nurse shot off her list of questions, "No, no, no, no…" was my response to all of them, and she jokingly said, "Well aren't you the poster child for chemotherapy. You should let people know this chemotherapy thing isn't that bad." I smiled and giggled. Then one of the nurses, who was helping another patient, turned to me and said, "Now don't get cocky because you never know."

I didn't respond, because again a comment like that does not require a response. She just doesn't get it. Unfortunately for her, she is mistaking positivity and faith for cockiness. But don't get me wrong, chemo is not fun.

Do I like the idea of poison running through my veins killing off healthy and unhealthy cells? Heck no. Do I wonder what kind of long-term effects the chemotherapy could have on my body? Of course, but this is the path I have chosen for my treatment. As a result, I choose to do what I can to keep the rest of me healthy, so that the side effects are minimal. There is countless evidence that chemotherapy side effects can effectively be minimized through the mind-body connection.

I can work on the mental aspect through faith, spirituality and a positive attitude. And, I can work on the physical aspect through exercise and smart nutrition choices.

I know some of you have either asked or wondered about the stage of my canser. To tell the truth, I have no idea. Well, I do have some idea, but I will not ask my doctor to give me a stage. When I was diagnosed with breast canser in 2007, I asked her what stage the canser was. She felt staging was an antiquated way of measuring canser and wouldn't provide a staging.

After that, I met with my oncologist for a treatment plan, and I was determined to find out what stage the canser was. So I asked, and she said it was Stage 1.

Now here is why I believe my surgeon's way of thinking. Stage 1 infiltrating ductal carcinoma with follow-up, adjuvant chemotherapy has an 85% to 90% five-year survival rate. (In the canser community, you are considered "cured" at the five-year mark.) If you do the math, I had a relatively small chance of canser coming back to disrupt my body.

They call the canser that recurred in my body metastatic breast canser, which means the original canser has spread to other areas of the body. (I hesitate giving out that information for those of you Internet junkies who will try and determine my fate by researching metastatic breast cancer.) For metastatic breast cancer, the five-year survival rate is much lower than 85% to 90%. But it is higher than 15% (the chance I had of it coming back), so I think I have a better chance of beating it than I did of getting it.

And since I am a numbers gal by trade, I know they are just numbers and as all analysts, C.P.As, politicians, etc., know, numbers can be manipulated to support any idea, theory or thought. It's all in the delivery of the numbers! More importantly, people defy the numbers all the time. And **my** numbers tell me to have 100% faith that I will be a very old survivor.

Holding my head high and fighting like a girl,
Sharyl

Earth Angels

> "Each time anyone comes in contact with us, they must become different and better people because of having met us. We must radiate God's love."
> —Mother Teresa

Monday, July 20, 2009

Well, I'm halfway through chemotherapy treatment. On Friday, I was blessed with one of the sweetest chemo nurses. They have rotating schedules, so it's not always the same one each time I go.

I am thoroughly convinced there are earth angels all around us and that people are put in our paths just when we need them, and I feel your prayers and they are being answered.

I decided I was going to go to chemo by myself so I could get some reading done on the book *God Said Yes*. If you ever feel a little sorry for yourself and need a reality check, I highly recommend reading Heather's story and considering the words she lives by: "Suck it up!"

I picked the chair in the corner of the back of the room, hoping no one else would come back there. After I sat down, I saw a jacket on the chair next to me, but no one was there. I thought, "Hopefully they are finishing up, and I will have this whole back area to myself." Then this couple about my parents' ages came back and the woman struck up a conversation right away. "So what kind of canser do you have?" A pang of irritation ignited in me at first. Can't she see that I'm reading? Do I look like I want to converse?

But when I looked up from my book and at this couple looking back at me with happy faces and smiling eyes, the irritation immediately drained, and I smiled and answered their question. Then, as couples sometimes do, together they told me about the kind of canser she is dealing with, each of them adding information to the other's sentences.

I spent about an hour and a half with them, and we talked about our families and jobs and things we like to do in our spare time. I knew they were placed in my path to spread hope and love when the man said to his wife and me, "You two girls need to always remain hopeful and positive and keep fighting." These are the kind of genuine people who make other people's lives better by just connecting with them for one hour.

And, as far as my little chemo nurse for the day, she was late getting to work and was eager to help the staff out, so she got an IV going on me, but not before complimenting my wig. (Now, that's a good way to start a needle poke—with a compliment.) She headed back to the nurses' station and asked if my drugs were ready and the other nurse said, "We haven't gotten her blood tests back yet, so hopefully you didn't stick her for nothing."

I could tell the nurse started to panic a little that she may have started my IV prematurely. I, however, knew that all would be fine. When she came back from the lab with my results, I could see the look of excitement and relief on her face, and she said to the other nurse, "Look at these numbers. They are fantastic!"

I didn't get a copy of my blood work from Friday, and I guess I don't really need it since my little nurse gave me two thumbs up and that's all the numbers I needed for the day. Besides, I had a conversation to get back to…

I hope you all had a great weekend and enjoyed the beautiful weather yesterday. This is my off week for chemo and next week Jason and I will be heading to Colorado to celebrate our 10th wedding anniversary. Thank you for the messages and your prayers. What a powerful testimony we will have to share.

Holding my head high and fighting like a girl,
Sharyl

†

Sharyl,

I love getting your updates as your words of wisdom make my day. You inspire me to be a better person. I think you should write a book yourself—you are reading everyone else's, but your entries could be a book!

Enjoy your time away with Jason! The two of you deserve it.

Keep fighting, smiling, praying and inspiring!
Jen

Confessions of a Canser Runner

Sunday, July 26, 2009

If I write a book, I decided today that it would be entitled "Confessions of a Canser Runner."* I've already shared some of my recent experiences while out jogging.

The first cool experience I had while out running was back in March of 2008. I decided I wanted to participate in the Susan G. Komen Race for the Cure and asked my brother Michael if he would be interested in running with me. He was, so I set out training for the run.

I had a goal to finish in the top five for the survivors. I gathered the times of the previous top five finishers from the last four years and figured out what time I needed to shoot for in order to obtain that goal.

One day back in March when I was out training, the South St. Paul cross country team was out for one of their runs. (Keep in mind that I had very short hair and wore a baseball hat or winter hat while out running, so I looked like I could still be undergoing treatment.) As the team approached, the young kids would smile and say "hi." But as one of the kids approached, he had the biggest smile on his face. When I got up closer to him, he raised his hand in the air to give me a high five. If that didn't give me motivation to stick with my goal, I don't know what would.

Sometimes nothing in particular happens while I'm out jogging; I just finish feeling good. Last week, the battery in my MP3 player died about a half mile into my jog. I was a little annoyed at first, but it's probably a good idea to run without music once in awhile. You can better gauge your breathing, and it's pretty cool to hear your feet on the pavement.

I had an encounter today that under any other circumstance would be considered kind of inappropriate. While I was out jogging, a man in a red truck passed by. I thought nothing of it until I approached the corner, and he was walking toward me.

He said, "Hi. I just wanted to stop and talk to you for a moment. I assume you are undergoing treatment for cancer?" I said, "Yes," and he shared that he was undergoing treatment for prostate cancer and had his last treatment tomorrow.

He said, "You look like you're obviously doing well," and asked for my name and if he could say a prayer for me. I said, "Why of course," and that I would do the same for him and went on my way to finish my jog. Like I said, under other circumstances, this approach would have been cause for concern, but it was just one survivor reaching out to another to share hope and faith.

But this is also one of the reasons you will find me wearing a wig out and about most of the time. I find it extremely irritating to get the "Aww, you have cancer" pity look from strangers. Your prayers I will gladly receive. Pity? No thanks. Don't need it!

I feel good. I am tolerating treatment well and other than the fact that I am bald :-(, you wouldn't have any indication I'm undergoing chemo. And I hope to continue this way and that my next scan in three weeks shows continued improvement on my way to remission. Have a blessed week.

Love,
Sharyl (Still holding my head high and fighting like a girl)

p.s. I took third for the Survivors in the 2008 Twin Cities Komen Race for the Cure 5K—only to be outrun by two seconds by a 44-year-old survivor and 45 seconds by a 51-year-old survivor.)

✝

Hi Sharyl,

I can't wait to read your book once you write one! Your messages are truly an inspiration to me! I love hearing about your faith, positive attitude and spirit and know they are the key to you beating this!

Love,
Leanne

*As Sharyl's journey continued, her attitude was defined by her cowgirl spirit, and "Fight with Cowgirl Spirit" was selected as the book title.

On Top of the World, Literally

"Courage is being scared to death but saddling up anyway."
—John Wayne

Thursday, July 30, 2009

Jason and I got back from our trip to Colorado today. We had a fantastic time! Yesterday, we did a zip-line adventure. I was terrified going into this outing. The first of six zip lines was described as the "bunny hill" and only 100-feet long, with a speed of 5 mph. As we got to the platform, I told Jason I didn't think I could do it. He said, "Of course you can," and I just shook my head no.

Jason volunteered to go first in our group of 11 people, which meant I would have to go second. After he zipped across the line, the guide looked at me to go next. My heart was racing, my hands were trembling and I thought to myself, "I could pull out my canser card, and I could probably even get a refund, so should I back out now?" (In the book *Crazy Sexy Cancer Tips*, Kris Carr explains that we should feel free to use our canser card at our discretion.)

As I looked at Jason across the other side of the canyon, I wondered how I could have let him convince me this would be a good idea! The guide looked at me again, and he knew I was scared. So he asked me to pick up my feet to see that the harness and cables would hold me. After I did that, he told me to step to the end of the platform and pick up my feet. Off I went! And, as much as I hate to admit it, I'm so glad Jason signed us up, because it was truly AWESOME!!!

I was having so much fun I couldn't wait to get to the next zip line. Our last was about 1,000-feet long and with the wind that day, we zipped down the canyon at a speed of about 45 to 50 mph. It was a truly magnificent and breathtaking experience. This picture is of Jason and me after we finished our 1,000-foot zip adventure. We were on top of the world, literally!

I also had a doctor's appointment today before the fourth of six chemotherapy cycles. My white cells and hemoglobin are great. I don't have protein in my urine, which is something else they have been monitoring while I'm on treatment, and my blood pressure is at 108/58 despite all the adrenaline rushes I experienced over the last couple of days.

My doctor excitedly told me about the success of the PARP Inhibitors. If you remember, I talked about them last month. They haven't received FDA approval yet, but they are trying to fast-track the approval process. The idea with the PARP Inhibitors is that for people with the BRCA1 and BRCA2 mutations, which most commonly trigger triple-negative breast canser, they would prevent the canser from developing.

This is great news for me! By fast-tracking the FDA process, they expect approval within four to five months. If it doesn't get fast-track approval, it will take about a year.

The doctor at the Mayo Clinic recommended that I possibly stay on one of the chemo drugs as a maintenance drug after my treatment—sort of as preventive measure. I am not sure how comfortable I am with that option, so fast-track approval of the PARP drugs would be a much better option for me, in my opinion.

God bless,
Sharyl

Cowgirl State of Mind

Survivor Lap Reflections

*There are three things that amaze me, four that I
do not understand: the way of an eagle in the sky,
the way of a snake on a rock, the way of a ship on the ocean,
and the way of a man with a woman.*
—Proverbs 30:18-19

Monday, August 3, 2009

Chemo went fine on Friday. My sweet, little Abby went with me. She likes to take care of her mom. She wasn't scared at all when the nurse put the needle in my arm and thought it was pretty cool to press the button on the blood pressure machine. Maybe we have a future nurse or doctor in the family.

This Friday, my family and I will be participating in the South St. Paul American Cancer Society Relay for Life. It will begin at 7 p.m., with the Luminaries Ceremony at dusk. This is a pretty cool event. They have a survivor lap, and last year they lined us up by number of years of survival and then had us newbies turn around and see all of the support behind us.

The only thing I am disappointed about in doing this year's lap is that instead of being in the row with the two-year survivors, I got bumped back to the beginning of the line. Oh well, I will work my way back toward that line.

Last year, I walked the survivor lap with my mom, which was pretty awesome, and I was thankful we were both here to walk it together. I saw old and new friends smiling and cheering us on. I almost felt like breaking into a sprint or a dance of joy in gratitude for being a survivor, but decided to cherish the moment instead.

It was hard to hold back the emotions though when I walked past my husband and my kids. When I looked at my kids, ranging from my big guy T, to my little guy Jake and my baby Abby and saw their smiles, I felt as though my heart was overflowing with love. Then I saw my husband, my rock, my true companion. I saw so much in his eyes in the moment when I walked past him. I saw his pride, joy, relief and, most importantly, I saw his love for me. Like many caregivers, Jason stands silently by my side as he and others rally around me to help me survive through these bumps.

He is what Kris Carr calls a co-survivor. The downside to being a co-survivor is they tend to stand alone. Jason stood by to watch the woman he married and loves transform before his eyes, not only physically but also mentally and emotionally. He watched as my body was transformed, as I lost and mourned my hair and as my hair and body "re-grew."

I think it is a pretty tough concept for a man to have to stand by and watch idly as someone he loves goes through pain or heartache. But what was most amazing to me is that although at times I felt like a mangled bald mess or a crazy-haired misfit, all he saw was the heart and soul of his best friend. So, in addition to walking for family and friends who have had canser, I walk in honor of my husband who fights the battle on the sidelines, never gives up, doesn't complain and most often does it alone.

I look forward to spending the evening with my family and friends again at this truly special event. Feel free to stop by and walk a lap in honor of a loved one, because one thing is certain, almost every life has been touched by canser.

Holding my head high and fighting like a girl,
Sharyl

Relay for Life—A Night of Hope

Saturday, August 8, 2009

Last night, the Relay for Life event was held at the South St. Paul Packer Activity Center. It was moved inside and proved to be a little warm, but 53 teams with 623 participants and many relay supporters attended.

It was again an amazing event, and the Relay committee deserves oodles of kudos for a great job in organizing, planning and executing it. As of this morning, the South St. Paul Area Relay for Life raised $132,566—not bad for this little town of which I am very proud to be a member.

The event was filled with so much faith and **HOPE**. "Hope" was the theme for the 25th Annual American Cancer Society Relay for Life. I spoke with friends relaying for family members who lost their battles with canser over the last year, and this event proved to be very emotional for them. My prayers go out to them, most especially my friends Julie, who lost her dad, and JulieAnne, who lost her mom, in the past year to canser. There were also powerful testimonies by survivors.

The testimony of Bethany Ames, another breast canser fighter and survivor, really hit home as she shared her story about diagnosis in April of 2007 (same as me) and her re-diagnosis in the spring of this year (just like me). She shared her fear in the early days after her diagnosis, when the crazy emotions are running rampant as we young wives and mothers deal with the worries about who is going to take care of our families if we die.

It brought me back to the dark hours and days of my initial diagnosis and re-diagnosis when my fears were getting the best of me. The first thought that popped into my head was, "Who is going to take care of my husband and children?" Jason is fully capable of raising our family without me, but with his firefighter schedule, he would need help, so my second thought was, "I have to find a wife for Jason before I die."

I know this sounds crazy, but unless you have experienced the dark fear and uncertainty of a terminal diagnosis, you can't imagine the irrational thoughts that go through your mind. But then, when the fear and irrational thoughts subside and you turn the corner and decide to go into fighter/survivor mode, it becomes "Either get behind me and believe in me or get the hell out of my way because I am on a mission."

I decided I will not give canser the power to defeat me or suck the joy from my life. I am going to raise my kids. I am going to see them graduate from high school and college. I am going to attend their weddings and become a grandma to all of their kids (not just Taylor's, since he will most likely make me a grandma sooner than Jake and Abby).

I am going to be my husband's wife for the next 40 to 50 years, and no one else is going to be the woman who makes him "Feel that Fire"—the Dierks Bently song he told me is his song for me. I have lots of things to do. I have many years of love, hope and messages to share with this world.

Another moving moment of the Relay was the survivor lap. We lined up again by years of survival in increments of five years. As we started our walk, my mom and I decided to walk together, even though we're in different groups. She is now a seven-year survivor. I was told that I'm still a two-year survivor, so I'm going with that. As we made our way around the track, there was constant clapping and cheering from the Relay supporters. As I approached my team and co-survivors, I saw my husband, my dad, Taylor, Jacob, my brother Michael, my sister-in-law Kristin, my nephew Luke, my sister Di, my nieces Emma, Grace and Liv, my teammates and friends Rhonda, Cindy, Laina, Darin, Karen, Linda, Kim and Buck. This overwhelmed me, and I started to tear up as I saw their smiles and heard their cheers for us.

As I turned the corner, I dropped my head a little. It was getting hard to hold back the tears and look people in the eyes. And then I thought, "You sign every CaringBridge post with 'Holding my head high,' get your head up now." So I did what I say at the end of every post; I held my head high.

As I turned the next corner I felt a hand on my back, and I turned to see the smiling face of Jacob's teacher for the upcoming school year. Then off to the right I saw three more smiling faces—Sal, Liz and Amy, friends from junior high, high school and Jefferson elementary. They were cheering and waving at me.

And then from out of the crowd, I heard "Mom! Mom!" and I turned to see my baby girl in her "My Mom Fights Like a Girl" shirt smiling and waving at me. My hope is that when she's all grown up, canser will be but a distant memory. Holding hands, my mom and I continued to make our way around the track. As I turned the last corner, I saw Brynn, one of Jacob and Abby's friends, and her dad Chad smiling at us. And, as I finished the lap, I was reminded by all those supporters that we don't fight this silly canser thing alone.

Thanks to all of you who are supporting, loving and praying for my family and me during this bump in the road. I can feel that I am being lifted up in your prayers, positive thoughts and belief for my healing and recovery. My cup runneth over, and I am truly blessed.

On Tuesday, I will have another scan to measure my healing, and **I believe** it will show that the canserous liver lesion is gone. I ask that you pray and believe in the same thing for me.

Holding my head high (I promise) and fighting like a girl!
Sharyl

†

Sharyl,

Once again you have amazed me with your words and the beautiful way you put them on paper. I too felt many of those same emotions you describe and was especially proud to walk with you, holding your hand as a gesture of hope and encouragement to you and me for the future and the day when we can walk at the end of the line.

Keep holding your head high, keep fighting like a girl and keep your FAITH! And, always remember your Father and I love you.

Mom

Cowgirl State of Mind

Tuesday, August 18, 2009

I've long considered myself a misplaced Southerner. The times when I've visited the South, I've always felt at home and that I would make a fine "Southern Belle." I love the southern style of hospitality, charm and, of course, the accent. And, I've longed to live on a ranch or farm with horses and lots of land.

While driving to the cabin this weekend, I took a detour and drove through some small towns in Minnesota. I love little towns; They are so inviting. I also love being able to drive for a long ways along farmland and undeveloped land. It breaks my heart when a for-sale sign goes up on undeveloped property just to build another housing development or another unnecessary shopping center!

I've told Jason that the day a fast-food restaurant opens up by our cabin, we are out of there. I would not be able to stand the idea of being able to run to McDonald's or Subway while at the lake.

When I was going through chemotherapy in 2007, I decided not to work while undergoing treatment, for many reasons. During that time, I was fortunate enough to spend long weekends and full weeks at the lake with my family.

I recently looked through my cabin journal and found how much I commented on nature and how healing it was for me. We spent a lot of our time on the water canoeing, swimming, boating and pedaling our paddle boat. We also went for lots of walks and four-wheeler rides. Northwest Wisconsin has some wonderful forest land that is quite amazing to take in.

After visiting Colorado, I realized I'm not a misplaced Southerner; What I really am is a cowgirl at heart. And cowgirls can be found anywhere in this beautiful country. I fell in love with the mountains, and Jason and I found a few spots when we were looking down from the mountains where we could retire someday.

I have always wanted to be able to call myself a cowgirl. Cowgirls are a tough breed. They may fall, but they always saddle up, hold their heads high and ride on. I thought you had to live on a ranch and own a horse to call yourself a cowgirl, but I've discovered being a cowgirl isn't about where you live, it's a state of mind.

In the closing page of the book, *Crazy Sexy Cancer Tips*, Kris Carr told me that I'm a "Cancer Cowgirl." I love the idea of being able to call myself a cowgirl. Here's how she describes a canser cowgirl:

"Cancer cowgirls are a divine order, a free-spirited bunch of powerful women who take charge as they gallop through life's obstacle course. We don't whisper, we ROAR. We are heavenly creatures full of sass and fireworks, dazzling warriors full of peace and fury. Cancer cowgirls past and present are survivors. Take the best and leave the rest."

She ends her book by reminding me to "Feel the ground beneath me and notice the groovy scenes as I hitchhike down the highway of one day at a time."

I don't know that I encompass all of those descriptions, but I certainly would like to attain them and live my life by them.

I'm hoping for the best of news from my doctor this week. Until then, I will hold my head high and keep fighting like a "cowgirl!"

Love,
Sharyl

†

Hi Sharyl,

I talked with your mom this morning during our Tuesday prayer group. Then I was able to read your journal and am blessed by your perspective and understanding.

I want you to know that you are in my prayers regularly and especially this week as you meet with your doctor. Many people are holding you up in prayer and asking for God's healing touch.

Hold on to those healing images and that cowgirl spunk! It makes you special and defines who you are. Remember too that we are all here to help hold you and your entire family up!

Blessings,
Pastor Terry

†

Sharyl,

Great entry today! One of the messages that I think we should all take to heart is that it's all about your "state of mind." You've chosen to view life in such a positive way, seeing beauty in things that most of us take for granted, and pausing long enough to appreciate God's blessings, big and small.

I'm looking forward to hearing about your meeting with your doctor. In the meantime, I'm sending you a big, virtual hug! :-)

Love,
Liz

Rainbows—A Mystical Beauty

The soul would have no rainbow had the eyes no tears.
—Native American Proverb

Thursday, August 20, 2009

When I went for my scan last week, I had been praying that the person who was going to insert the IV would get the needle in on the first try. I tried a different approach with my appointment, going later in the day, so I would only have fasted for three hours versus 12 with an early appointment.

I talked with the tech and explained to her that she could only use my left arm and that even though the vein in the bend of my arm looks good, I have yet to have a tech successfully get the needle in because of scarring to the veins. I told her I'm not against going in my hand. They don't like to go in the hands because the veins are smaller, and it can hurt a little more than some of the other veins. But it beats having your arm strangled for 20 minutes, being poked numerous times and looking at the bruising left behind.

So the hand it was! Successful on the first attempt, and I was happy. Then she came back into the room and said, "We are going to take a couple more pictures." My heart sank and panic crept into my head. My mind started racing. Why would they need to take extra pictures? What did they see? Has it spread? Has it grown? Are there new areas? Do I have the H1N1 virus? What the heck is going on???

My faith was shaken, and I was unsettled. It was the waiting game all over again. It brought me back to the fear I had while waiting for the biopsy results. I lost it Wednesday night last week and yelled to my mom. It's a good thing she loves me unconditionally.

I had a pity party for myself, and became a bit frantic. I waited Thursday, Friday and Monday for the doctor to call with bad news. Every time my phone rang, my heart raced in anticipation.

I was playing ping-pong in my head with all of the "what ifs." I spent time in prayer trying to stay calm, and then I wrote a CaringBridge post on Tuesday, just getting some of my thoughts out on "paper" helped to calm me down. Receiving messages of hope and prayers from family and friends also helped me to stay calm, focused and faith-filled. However, I couldn't wait any longer. I put in a call to my doctor's office for the results. The anxiety was not doing me any good.

Thursday of last week, my mom sent me an email that included a picture of rainbow. It reminded me of the rainbow encounters I have been experiencing over the last few months. As described by author Donald Ahrens in his text *Meteorology Today*, a rainbow is "one of the most spectacular light shows observed on earth." I would have to agree.

Whenever I witness a rainbow, I feel like a little kid. I excitedly point it out to whoever is around me at the time. I thought about some of the special rainbow sightings I have recently witnessed. One was in January, when I pointed a rainbow out to Jason while we were on our way to church for a neighbor's memorial service.

I guess I don't remember ever seeing a rainbow in January in Minnesota, but as we made our way to the service, the rainbow extended over the church as if Deb and God were telling her family and friends that she was happy and that they were smiling down upon us with their colorful smiles.

I would see rainbow reflections throughout my house or on pages of books I was reading created by a glass of water, or whatever else may create the lighting of rainbows. When Jason and I flew to Colorado, as we took off into the air, I saw off in the distance that we were approaching a rainbow. I pointed it out to Jason and before we knew it, we were flying through its bow. It was quite an awesome experience to be that close to a rainbow and experience one of God's awesome gifts up close and personal.

When we came back from dinner one night, three deer were eating their own dinner in the yard of our rented cabin. We watched as they ate, and they didn't even seem to mind our presence. I looked off into the sky and saw a rainbow to accompany the splendor of our deer-watching.

Rainbows are quite a mystical beauty, and my heart fills with happiness whenever I see one. They are like a promise of hope and faith—that we may experience rain in our lives, but some of the most spectacular beauty is created as a result of the rain!

The nurse called me Tuesday afternoon to say that the CT scan showed good news. There is no progression of canser in my body and the liver lesion is continuing to decrease. PRAISE GOD!

At my appointment today, my blood work was described by my doctor as "perfect." My blood pressure is 108/62 and the kidney test was good, so I am still tolerating everything very well.

Tomorrow is another round of chemo. The next scan in six weeks will show an even better report of a canser-free body! (Still not sure why they needed to take a few more pictures but my doctor told me I can usually call the next day for results. Good to know for the future.)

Holding my head high and fighting like a cowgirl! Yeeeeeeehaw!
Sharyl

10th Annual
Caylin Saver Memorial Open

August 22, 2009

Oak Marsh Golf Club
Oakdale, Minnesota

Proceeds to Benefit Camp Discovery
for Children with Skin Disorders

Dinner, Golf & Prizes - $100
Dinner Only - $25

Double-Start Tee Times Begin at 12 p.m.
Dinner at 6 p.m.

Music by the Lid Twisters

RSVP to Sharyl/Jason Saver or Dianna Lilla

Hope to see you at this year's event!

Breast Cancer 101

Friday, August 28, 2009

I have successfully completed 10 rounds of chemotherapy, and am now done with five of eight cycles. I think I said before that I had to do six cycles, but I was wrong.

Today, I thought I would give you my breast canser 101 knowledge and how it relates to me and the canser that developed in my body. Keep in mind that I received my education by living it rather than in a classroom or as an intern, and I have participated in treatments and clinical trials as opposed to diagnosing, researching and prescribing. So, my knowledge is not approved by the American Medical Association, but I think I'm passing with flying colors.

I've written a lot about the fact that I have triple-negative breast canser, and I'm sure some of you are wondering what that means. Before someone is diagnosed with breast canser, a biopsy is done to determine if the suspicious lump that appeared on a mammogram, MRI or ultrasound is canserous. The tumor is then tested to determine if it is positive or negative for estrogen receptors, progesterone receptors and HER2/neu, a growth-promoting protein.

Depending on the outcome, this will allow the doctor to determine how to best treat the canser—particularly what treatments and drugs can and cannot be used.

In the canser that developed in my body, the tumor tested negative for all three. During the initial diagnosis, it did not really change any of the treatment plans except that there would be no benefit in taking a proven HER2/neu-protein-targeted follow-up drug to prevent recurrence. It also was determined that I have a mutated gene that researchers have found increases a woman's lifetime risk for developing breast and ovarian canser.

In my research of triple-negative breast canser and how it relates to the BRCA1 genetic mutation, I found that the BRCA1 mutation typically results in a triple-negative tumor. I have also discovered that triple-negative tumors can be aggressive and hard to treat because they do not respond to proven chemotherapy drugs like Tamoxifin and Herceptin in the way that hormone-positive and HER2/neu tumors do.

This is where in my case the PARP Inhibitors come into play. There was a lot of attention at the Oncology Summit my doctor attended in June about the success of PARP Inhibitors in treating triple-negative tumors in people who have the BRCA1 and BRCA2 genetic mutations.

When I first met with her after being diagnosed with a recurrence of canser, my doctor told me that she could not offer me a cure; she could only treat it. By treating it, she said they would put it in remission and "when" it came back, they would treat it again, and "when" it came back again at some point, I would need to be ready to make some decisions. And, she said I should make sure that I have all of my "affairs in order."

I asked her why I couldn't believe that I would be one of those people who defy the odds and put the canser in remission for many years. I have heard of two men who had colon canser and when the canser came back in their livers, they did chemo and wiped it out, and that was over five years ago for both of them. She said I could find hope in that, but that colon and breast canser are very different.

As my doctor told me I could be hopeful, she pointed to Dianna and said, "But it's my job, her job and your husband's job to be realistic." Well, I think she would be hard-pressed to get my husband to give up hope and be a pessimist. If she thinks she can't offer me a "cure," that's fine, but that would assume she thinks she offered me a cure back in 2007, and obviously she didn't do such a hot job on that one.

She doesn't cure, GOD does. I'm not sharing this so that I will get a bunch of negative comments about my doctor because that's not what I want to hear. I'm sharing this because I feel that every time I see her, her attitude changes and the disbelief she had in the numbers and in me are changing. Before I started treatment, I asked her if I could exercise during chemotherapy, and she chuckled a little and said, "Well you can certainly try but if you are going to work during treatment and then keep up with the activities of two younger children, I really don't think you will have the energy."

She now seems to be very entertained by the fact that I am still jogging, working, coaching soccer, climbing mountains, zipping down canyons, participating in the Relay, hosting a charity golf tournament, not to mention being a mom to two young kids and sending one off to college. And, I'm doing all of this while keeping my white cells at levels that are well into the normal range.

When the research person asked my doctor, "Did you know Sharyl went mountain climbing in Colorado?" my doctor said, "I know, and it's great that she feels good enough to do it." At my last appointment, I mentioned to her that I don't have the same endurance and stamina I did three months ago when I exercise, and she laughed and rolled her eyes at me.

I know some of you have asked if I'm overdoing it by exercising, and I just want you all to know that when I don't feel full of energy and when my body aches, I actually feel 100 times better after jogging. (Not to mention that my dog runs in circles when I get home from work, waiting for me to get ready to go for a jog.) So, the answer to that would be a resounding "NO." And it makes me feel so good to hear from people when they tell me that I motivate them to stay on track with their exercising. (I will send you my personal training bill in the mail.)

Last week when I was at the doctor's office, they had the magazine *Caring4Cancer* and Lance Armstrong was on the cover. In the article "Racing toward a cure for a cancer," Lance said that before knowing his own fate, he declared himself a canser survivor, not a canser victim.

Lance was diagnosed with testicular canser in 1996, and by the time he was diagnosed, it had already spread to his brain and lungs, which would mean it had metastasized. He was given a 50% survival rate but "his will to live was bigger than the disease itself." I embody the same belief he has in that "attitude is everything...cancer is tough, but you can never lose hope."

I know that I will defy the odds as well, and that I am and will continue to be a survivor for many years. I will be the person my doctor can use to offer hope to another person facing a recurrence diagnosis.

Holding my head high and fighting like a cowgirl,
Sharyl

†

To My Favorite Daughter-in Law,
Sharyl, remember that Jesus has come to help you, and He will be by your side all the way. And, we love you and will be by your side all the way. We are looking so forward to the day you find out the canser is gone!

Love,
Diane

So Long, Soda

Tuesday, September 8, 2009

I mentioned the article I read about Lance Armstrong the other day, but I'd never heard of him before he was diagnosed with canser. I remember the day I learned of his diagnosis in 1996. My boss at the time was very big into cycling, and he and a colleague were talking about Lance's diagnosis of testicular canser and that it had spread to his brain and lungs. My boss said his chances of making it were pretty slim.

I don't know why I remember this conversation so well. Maybe it was because he was close to my age, but I remember sitting in my boss' office thinking he was going to defy the odds; He was going to survive. I just knew it. I thought of my Aunt Maxine, who at the time was a two-time canser survivor and had twice been told by her doctors to have her affairs in order. So in my mind, canser was something people could beat.

I've heard that canser in young adults 20 to 40 years of age can be aggressive and often harder to treat. But in my opinion, if you have prepared your body well, you are also in your prime "fighting" health. You have made it out of the puberty and teen years, when your body was still developing and growing. And, during the young adult stage, you have built up an immune system, your endurance has developed and if you have stayed active after high school, you have continued to develop your strength as well. So, in my mind (again not approved by the AMA), you are at your best to fight against an attack on your body.

I know some people felt the same strong belief about me—that I was going to beat this—when they heard of the recurrence. For some of you, it may have taken a little longer, but I know you believe it now, and I'm grateful for your faith in my healing.

I have also been trying in so many ways to make positive changes in the way I eat, but I don't always eat exactly the way I want to, and I still make poor choices. I do buy into the concept that sugar feeds canser and have taken a lot of sugar and anything that contains sugar substitutes out of my diet. And, since I have a genetic mutation that increases my risk for canser, I will do what I need to do to prevent it from ever developing again.

One of the reasons I buy into the sugar thing is that one of the tools used to diagnose canser in a body is a PET scan—a test in which they inject sugar into your body. The sugar goes to the canserous areas and reacts by lighting up on the scan. Hmmm. So long, soda. It was fun while it lasted.

I tried for a few weeks to go vegan. That is a tough commitment, especially since one of the main staples in my diet is yogurt, which keeps my white cells in the normal range. So, I strive for a balance of vegan, vegetarian and, occasionally, free-range meat. I haven't perfected my diet, but I'm working on it.

I also think that at times it's important to just enjoy a piece of cake or treat in celebration of a birthday or an out-of-town relative visiting. Or an occasional "just because." And after chemo, when I am ravenous and can eat anything in sight, I try not to beat myself up when I fall off the sugar or meat wagon. And when I feel like having wine during my off week, I plan to enjoy it. The doctor at Mayo told me, "Wine for medicinal purposes is just fine." (Besides, I have to believe red wine is much less taxing on your body than the poison of chemotherapy drugs.)

I've also let go of feeling the need to be hard on myself when I exercise and instead just enjoy the jog or walk, along with my surroundings or companions, and appreciate the fact that I can exercise. (Remember my post about my dog a few months back?)

For instance, a few weeks ago when I was jogging up the hill by our house, it was quite warm and my dog and I had had enough. I thought to myself, "I don't have anything to prove, so let's just walk it the rest of the way." With his tongue hanging out of his mouth, Blazer looked up at me in appreciation. But he was the first one to follow me around the house to go for a jog the next day.

My friend Sandy told me after my initial diagnosis she believes God has big plans for me. God has big plans for all of us, but maybe his plan for me is to help change the face of canser—to demonstrate by living with hope, prayer, positive attitude, faith and healthy choices, that I am a resource to other canser survivors.

Holding my head high and fighting like a cowgirl,
Sharyl

†

Hey Sharyl!
I saw a rainbow on the way to work today, and I immediately thought of you! Keep fighting girl! We are behind you today and every day.

Jared, Jess and Ava

The Fine Print

Friday, September 11, 2009

Yesterday, I saw my doctor and the conversation went as usual, at first. Weight is steady, blood pressure is great, no protein in my urine, white cells are "perfect" (her words not mine). And then she said, "I am not sure if you understood this or not about the trial because I was not aware of it either, but this trial has the cycles of chemotherapy going on for an indefinite period of time."

Uh, what? Umm, NO, I was not aware of that "fine print." I told her the schedule they gave me back in May had the chemotherapy running through October 30th. She also told me that if for some reason the liver tumor was still there, they could do radiofrequency ablation to zap the last of it out of there.

When I went to Mayo, the doctor suggested perhaps staying on one of the drugs as a maintenance drug, but never mentioned that the trial would go on indefinitely. I think their (the trial people) thought process for staying on the trial indefinitely is "no matter what, the canser is going to recur at some point and the longer you stay on chemo, the better your chances of it not coming back."

My doctor said typically the reasons for stopping chemo are that either the canser has progressed beyond control, or your body is not tolerating the side effects well and you need a break. She said she doesn't see the latter happening to me, so she suggested maybe staying on the trial for a total of one year. I told her I'm not sure about this, and we should see how the next two scans look and then make decisions about my treatment plan.

I'm not obligated to stay on the trial. And I just don't know about torturing my veins and body with three very strong chemo drugs. Besides, PARP Inhibitors should have FDA approval within a year.

So much to think about, and I kind of felt the wind was being taken out of my sails a little yesterday. It's a lot to take in, digest and sort through in my mind. It did seem like my doctor is feeling more hopeful because she said, "I would like to know what they consider an indefinite period of time." As if she was thinking, "We can't keep her on chemo for the next 40 years!"

Always holding my head high and fighting like a cowgirl,
Sharyl

†

Sharyl,
You amaze me with your grace and strength. Try to think of this chemo news like another bump in the road. You can and will get over it, and you will find a clear path that's best for your body and soul.

You have taught all of us, by example, the power of positive thinking and enjoying life as it comes. Know that you are changing the face of cancer in a good way. You give such hope to others to keep on fighting, to keep on praying and believing, to know that there is always hope, to never give up, to look for life's rainbows and sunshine and to feel God's presence in our lives.

Karen

Pounding Out Negativity

Wednesday, September 16, 2009

I haven't been out for a jog with my dog for over a week, but yesterday we were finally able to make time to get out together for a quick jog. Whenever I jog, it helps me to clear my head, put life in perspective and reenergize my focus. So yesterday we jogged away together, pounding out negativity, fear, frustration and confusion with every step.

Right before I was told chemo could go on indefinitely, I had just shared with a friend that I was having a hard time looking in the mirror. I only have a few eyelashes left, and my once full eyebrows are now sparse. I am not a plucker, and I like my full eyebrows—I don't care what Cosmo says—and I am not that good at applying eyeliner. We ended the conversation by saying that in about eight weeks my hair would start to be in full bloom, and I would be on the road to looking like me again. I don't enjoy wearing a wig, hat or a bandana on a regular basis, but I can't let the fact that my reflection in the mirror frustrates me influence my decision about this trial. Yet I also am not ready to make any decisions with respect to the trial until after the next two scans.

If I do decide to stay on chemo, I'd have a slight interruption since I would most likely need to have a port inserted. My left arm veins will have a hard time tolerating much more abuse. It took three attempts the other day to get a vein and one popped, which hurt like a son of a gun. I think it (the vein) was just being stubborn because it (the vein) also was annoyed with the news.

The reason this trial goes on indefinitely is because it is a trial; It is not an approved treatment plan. They are still trying to determine the best course of action for these three drugs. All of the drugs are approved for the treatment of metastatic breast canser—it is just the combination and the duration that have not been final ized. And since I tolerate chemo exceptionally well, my doctor doesn't see any reason to pull me off the trial.

I intend to pray on the decision, and I know that God will lead me to the right answer. I believe remission is in my future and, in the meantime, I will practice patience and continued faith while that is being revealed.

God bless,
Sharyl

†

Sharyl,
You are truly an amazing woman. You have that great gift not only of outward beauty but also of inward beauty, strength and faith.

I know what a blow it was for you to get the news about more chemo, but the way you are able to adjust and rely on trust and hope speaks volumes for your faith. You were fortunate to find your recurrence at a very early stage, and it could just be that you are defying the odds and this is something new for them.

You are truly a miracle in progress. I am in such awe of your determination and the beautiful way you have of lifting everyone else up in your time of pain. I know God is using you. Listen for His words to you and then respond.

Love You,
Mom

Hope Does Not Disappoint

Monday, September 21, 2009

I was reading a devotion the other day, and it referred to a scripture that gave me much peace at another difficult time in my life:

> *"And we rejoice in the hope of the glory of God. Not only so, but we also rejoice in our sufferings, because we know that suffering produces perseverance, perseverance character and character hope. And hope does not disappoint us, because God has poured out His love into our hearts by the Holy Spirit, whom He has given us."*
> —Romans 5:2-5

I shut my bible after reading that scripture and thought, "I have done this before, and I can do it again."

Nine years ago, my husband and I put our faith in God that He would fulfill our hope to have a child free from epidermolysis bullosa (EB), the skin disorder that took our sweet sweet, little, baby girl Caylin from us when she was just six weeks old.

On the drive home from the hospital after Caylin had passed, Jason turned to me and said, "I think God put you and me together so that I would still be able to be a father." I was very blessed to have fallen in love with a man who not only loved me, but also loved Taylor as if he were his own.

Jason and I had also come to learn we were both genetic carriers for EB, and we had a 25% chance with each pregnancy of having a child with EB. I liked to refer to it as having a 75% chance of having a child without EB. It is another genetic mutation in my body that doesn't cause any physical problems for me, but can be passed on to my children. And, when you meet that one-in-a-million person (or so they told us) who also has a mutation in the same gene line, it can result in your child having EB. (Again, more medical knowledge than I cared to learn.)

So, we had to rely on faith when choosing to have more children. A few months after Caylin died, we decided to try again. We got pregnant but unfortunately that pregnancy resulted in a miscarriage. I desperately wanted another child. When Jason proposed to me a couple of years earlier, right after I said yes, I said, "Can we have a baby right away?"

We tried again after the miscarriage and thankfully the pregnancy was successful. After making it through the first trimester, we decided to have a genetic test done by amniocentesis to determine whether or not the baby was affected by EB. Amnios cannot be done until at least 16 weeks and then you wait another three weeks for the results. So, I would be halfway through my pregnancy before I knew whether or not the baby was EB-free.

While waiting for the news, I was growing a little anxious. My cousin had sent me a letter and included the above verse in it. I concentrated on those words. I put the verse on a sticky note and in my planner so that I would see it every day as a reminde to stay calm and peace-filled.

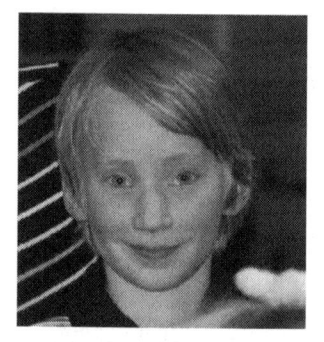

The doctor called me about three weeks after the test and said that the baby was EB-free. I asked her if she knew the sex, and she shared with me that the baby was a boy. And that's the story of our great news of Jacob. (I have an awesome butterfly story to share from that day but it will have to wait.)

I had always wanted to have lots of kids and pictured myself with at least four kids, maybe five. Perhaps it was irresponsible on our part, but I believed God knew the desires of our hearts and our hope for just one more child. We decided to try again and again got pregnant. We were so happy but then after the initial elation, the fear started to creep in along with all of the what ifs...

One day, very early in the pregnancy, I was working out during lunch and felt a gush. I thought to myself, "No, no, no, please God no, not again." I went to the locker room hoping it was a weak pregnancy bladder; but that wasn't the case. I quickly grabbed my stuff, left the gym and called my doctor's office. The nurse who answered said, "It sounds like you are having a miscarriage."

I was devastated. The nurse told me to come into the office in the morning for an ultrasound. I called my mom and hysterically told her I was having another miscarriage. She didn't even know I was pregnant. We were going to wait to tell people until after we had gotten the EB-free results.

Overnight, I just felt that this was not a miscarriage and that the baby was going to be fine in so many ways. When I arrived at the doctor's office the next morning, the same nurse I spoke with the day before was there to do the ultrasound. As she got ready to do the test, she said, "I don't expect that we will see a heartbeat."

I ignored her negativity. It amazes me how so many people in the medical field have such little faith. You would think being surrounded by medical miracles every day that they would be the most faith-filled people around. Childbirth alone is a medical miracle that blows my mind.

As she moved the wand around she said, "Well, will you look at that? There's a heartbeat." I was overjoyed. About a month later, we were able to have the genetic test and once again I concentrated on the scripture above that great news would be revealed. We didn't wait to tell people about the baby—we thought the more prayer covering the better.

About three weeks after the procedure, the clinic called and said the baby was EB-free. I again asked for the sex and was told we would be having another little girl. I knew that her name would be Gabrielle, meaning "God is my strength," or Abigail, "My father's joy." Her daddy decided she would be Abigail.

Even though my husband and I were enduring one of life's most painful losses, we knew God understood the desires of our hearts and wanted us to be happy. And He knew of our hope of expanding our family and He would fulfill that hope because hope does not disappoint.

And so I know that it will be revealed again, that although canser produces suffering, through that suffering, it will produce perseverance and through perseverance, character, which will in turn lead to hope, and that hope will not disappoint, and once again great news will be revealed.

After I shut my bible, I changed into my jogging clothes and with Blazer, I pounded out these thoughts while out for a run. Next week, I will have another scan. And, as I wait for more great news, I will keep holding my head high and fighting like a cowgirl.

Have an awesome week. God bless,
Sharyl

Rainbows Comes in Many Shapes and Forms

*"The way I see it, if you want the rainbow,
you gotta put up with the rain."*
—Dolly Parton

Thursday, October 1, 2009

I've been hearing a song on the radio that I would consider "bubble gum country" called "Outside My Window" by Sarah Buxton. It's a cute song about friends, laughter, beautiful music, good news and the rainbows right outside our windows.

Whenever we hear it, Abby and I break into song and dance. It makes me smile and as I am singing along, it reminds that I have rainbows in many shapes and forms in my life.

Today, my doctor and I went over the results of my CT scan from Monday. The liver lesion is holding steady at 1.3 cm. This may not sound like great news, but I feel good about what we discussed. Since the liver lesion is holding steady, she said we have options. One is to stay on the trial. The other is to have localized treatment to the liver with either: surgery, radio-frequency ablation or SIRS, a new radiation treatment I learned about on "The Doctors."

I will have a PET scan sometime in the next week or so and then meet with the liver surgeon to discuss my options. If I'm a candidate for a localized liver treatment, I would possibly be done with chemo as soon as next week and have the localized treatment in early December. I would need to be off chemo for eight weeks before having localized treatment.

I also asked my doctor if it is possible that the area showing up on the CT scan is not canserous? She said "Yes" and that it is a definite possibility that the 1.3 cm lesion on my liver is scarring from chemo. The CT scan only shows shading of things in your body; It doesn't show whether or not they are canserous. That's where the PET scan comes in.

I feel good about this and think it is just one more step in the direction toward remission. Thank you so much for all your prayer covering. Keep looking for the rainbows in your lives.

Holding my head high and fighting like a cowgirl.

God bless,
Sharyl

✝

Sharyl,

I want you to know that you and your family are in my thoughts and prayers every day! When I talk about you to my friends and family, I start out by saying, "I have this friend who is the most positive person I have ever met.

If I'm having a bad day or become frustrated with something, you automatically come to mind, and I say to myself, "Just stop thinking about the negative and think about how to handle life's bumps like Sharyl does."

I think God is talking to all of us through the words you share and telling us to listen with our hearts to what you say and do. I owe you a thank you for opening my eyes to see God in a different light. Because of you, I have joined a church, and I look at my life with such a different perspective.

Thank you for being our living angel,
Jody

The Power of Pink

Tuesday, October 6, 2009

With it being Breast Canser Awareness (BCA) month, we are seeing pink everywhere. I know some breast canser survivors get annoyed with the whole pink thing, and that's okay. I, however, am not offended one bit by all the pink on display this month. As I'm sure many of you witnessed over the weekend, the NFL showed its support for BCA with players, coaches and officials wearing pink on their hats, arms, hands and feet.

I stopped at Caribou this morning to pick up some Amy's Blend coffee, which supports BCA. I also heard a commercial for a bagel store donating to BCA. I was watching "The Doctors" for a little bit again yesterday, and the audience members were all wearing pink Avon Walk for a Cure t-shirts for the event that took place over the weekend in New York.

There are many events throughout the month to promote BCA for research and support. Breast canser tends to get a lot of attention for the simple reason that it is one of the most common types of canser in women. And the advancements that have been made in breast canser research have helped the treatment of other types of cansers.

There is a statistic that one in eight women will develop breast canser. Three years ago, I was out to dinner with my group of friends from high school; We call ourselves "Dinner Club." There are nine of us, and somehow that statistic came up in conversation. A comment was made that one of us could be the one in eight.

Two of my friends looked at me and said, "We've been meaning to talk to you about this. When are you getting a mammogram?" They knew that both my mother and my maternal aunt are breast canser survivors. I said I had seen my doctor in August and she didn't see any rush to get one, but she said if I wanted to, I could get a baseline before I was 40.

To tell the truth, I didn't see the rush to get a mammogram. I exercise four to five days a week, eat well, nursed my kids and had a child young. The checklist was all checked off, except for a couple of items, and I didn't see myself as a likely candidate to develop breast canser.

So, I pushed aside their concern and went on with my life until that morning in 2007, when my little Jacob came in to give me a hug. He gently put his head on my chest, and as much as I enjoyed that hug, panic set in because it felt where he had laid his head, and I discovered a lump. I thought about it all day long. I touched it again and again.

The hug came on a Monday morning. By Wednesday morning, I couldn't push it aside anymore and made an appointment to see the doctor. At the visit, she felt the lump and didn't seem too concerned, but considering the family history thought it best that I have a mammogram. The next day, after I completed the mammogram, they wanted to do an ultrasound. "Oh crap," I thought. (I think I probably said something worse but will clean it up for you.)

As the tech was going over and over the lump, measuring and taking pictures, my heart was racing faster and faster. I saw her measure something and on the screen it said 6 cm. Now I was really freaking out. Jason was working that day, so my mom came with me. In the room, I felt like a scared little girl and asked the tech to please go get my mom.

She said she just needed to finish up and then she would get her. She finished the ultrasound and got my mom. While, my mom and I were alone in the room I said, "Mom, I am going to die; it's 6 cm." My mom, trying to hold it together, was thinking, "What the heck? 6 cm—how did it get that big?"

The doctor on staff at the radiology clinic came in to talk to me and said, "The lump looks suspicious. We need to do a biopsy, but the good news is that it's pretty small—it's only about 1 cm." I was somewhat relieved. When I mentioned to the tech that I thought it was 6 cm, she said, "You were asking me many questions that I couldn't answer, but I could have answered that one."

The next day, I went in for a biopsy and found out the following week that the lump was canserous. For many reasons, I decided to have a bilateral mastectomy and breast reconstructive surgery at a later date. When I woke up from surgery, the first words out of my mouth were, "Did it spread to my lymph nodes?" The nurse assured me that it hadn't.

I was overjoyed—the kind of joy you feel when you hold your newborn baby in your arms—but made her tell me at least three more times. As I was being wheeled from recovery to the hospital room, I saw my husband, my dad, my mom and my father-in-law. They all had smiles as big as Texas. I locked eyes with my dad and will never forget the look of pure joy that filled them.

Because of my age (36 at the time) and the grade of the tumor (three of three), which meant it was fast-growing, it was recommended that I follow the standard preventative chemotherapy treatment. This should kill any stray canser cells that may have gotten loose in my blood stream.

And that should do it. I'd be able to put this canser thing behind me and move on with my life. So, I did what I was told like a good little girl who doesn't like to break the rules. Was it the right decision? I really can't answer that, and it really doesn't matter. I can only deal with the here and now. And the here and now is I am in a different place than I was two years ago.

Two years ago, I didn't think I had to change anything in my life because of canser. I felt somewhat invincible because I had my breasts removed and did chemotherapy. I thought I could do whatever I wanted and it wouldn't come back. I was protected. Besides, I had been dealt enough in my life; I felt I was somehow exempt from any further heartache, pain or suffering.

But, life doesn't work that way. And every day, in the back of my mind, I was waiting, waiting for the day it would come back. Although I consider myself a very positive person and know that you need to have faith and believe in the power of your thoughts and words, I kept waiting. The word recurrence was a daily thought in my mind. Did this cause canser to develop in my body again? No, but did I help myself by giving in to stress and worry every day? No, absolutely not!

My point is that however the canser developed again is somewhat insignificant. What *is* important is how I respond to it, how I use it to benefit others and how I can better myself as I grow through it.

My doctor told me the other day that the trial ends with progression. I said, "I'm not looking for progression." She replied, "I know you are not looking for progression, which is why we look for other options as well."

As I was watching "The Doctors" yesterday and saw the pink audience, I said to myself, "Survival is my only option." Then as I watched the NFL game last night and saw pink everywhere, again I thought, "Survival is my only option." And in my devotional book focused on canser treatment, I read the words, "Your canser is not a permanent condition." I am re-wording it to say, "My healing is a permanent condition!"

So, as we are inundated with pink this month, please don't cringe. Pink is the color of universal love and provides a feeling of caring, tenderness, self worth and love. The symbolic Christian meaning of pink is joy and happiness. In the breast canser world, it is a reminder to do your self exams and, if you are over the age of 35, ask for a mammogram. It's a great baseline!

Holding my head high and fighting like a cowgirl,
Sharyl

†

Sharyl,

What a wonderful message to women about getting a mammogram. I have been a strong believer in the value of mammograms since it was only because of a mammogram that my canser was found. When it did not show up on the ultrasound, it was only because of my family history that a biopsy was done.

So, I say to all women out there, you need to be your own advocate because no one else will. Make sure you do your self-exams and get those mammograms, especially if you have any family history. Also even though it is rare, remember men can get breast canser too. So let's celebrate Breast Cancer Awareness month and wear pink.

Sharyl, bless you for the inspiration you are to everyone you encounter. I know God has great plans for you in this journey you are on. Bless you and keep fighting like a cowgirl.

Love you,
Mom

p.s. Your dad also loves you and keeps you in his prayers.

God's Been Good to Me

Hope deferred makes the heart sick,
but a longing fulfilled is a tree of life.
—Proverbs 13:12

Tuesday, October 13, 2009

Oh, happy day!!! I am going to just get right to it. I am kind of speechless; Shocking, I know. My doctor called me with the results of my PET scan.

It is with the utmost praise that I say, "MY LIVER IS CANSER-FREE!!!"

My doctor did say the lymph nodes under my arm are faintly lighting up as very small areas on the PET scan. But she also said it could be just inflammatory. I believe that I am canser-free and in remission. My doctor and I decided I will continue on chemo for another couple of months or so. I will have a CT scan the first week of November after this next round of chemo and then have another PET scan in December.

In the letter my cousin gave me about nine years ago, she also included the above scripture, and it too provided peace during our sadness and uncertainty.

As always, holding my head high and fighting like a cowgirl!

God bless,
Sharyl

p.s. I'm listening to Keith Urban right now, and the song "God's Been Good to Me" is on. How appropriate.

†

Sharyl,
Praise The Lord for Hope Realized!!!!!!!!!!!!!
Loréal

†

Sharyl,
I am praising God today for your remission, your attitude and that I got to read your journal! The way you walk out your faith is amazing to me. In an odd way, I am thankful epidermolysis bullosa brought us together.
Laurie

†

Praise Jesus! That is fabulous news! My heart is doing little jumps for you! Let this be the end to your canser. FOREVER.

Hope, faith and love from another survivor,
Lori

†

YESSSSS!!!!! Yay God! :-)
Emily

On My Way to Being a Real Cowgirl

Cheerleaders Never Give Up Hope

Tuesday, October 20, 2009

I have talked about being a cheerleader when I was in high school, how important it was to me and how it helped shape me into the person I am today. But, I almost didn't try out for cheerleading. I missed the first day of clinics, and my brother Michael came home and said, "I heard you weren't at the cheerleading clinics."

I don't know why he cared, but if it weren't for him I would have missed out on something that was a defining experience in my life. As it turned out, two cheerleaders who had crushes on him devoted the next afternoon solely to helping me get caught up. Thanks, Michael!

When it came to my tryouts, I was so loud I even surprised myself. My science teacher, who was one of the judges, said, "Well, you can finally put your big mouth to use." (I had a problem of "talks too much" on my report cards and at conferences.)

Cheerleading truly fit my personality. I was bubbly, loud and energetic. It was such an awesome experience to stand in front of my classmates at a Friday night football game and to cheer on the ice at a hockey game. (I can proudly say that I skated on the ice at a high school hockey tournament.) Or to get everyone excited at a Friday afternoon pep fest, and I can't leave out the soccer and basketball games and what came to be one my favorite sports to cheer, wrestling. South St. Paul cheerleaders back in the day had the unique experience of cheering for all fall and winter sports.

With the advancement of Title 9, which is awesome, cheerleaders in states like Minnesota have become a thing of the past. I can't tell you how many times in the past five years when I have been at a South St. Paul varsity event that someone of my age group says, "Where are the cheerleaders?" followed by "Where is the band?" When I was in high school, the band and cheerleaders were a visible and vocal presence at all football and hockey games, as well as most soccer and basketball games. Call it school spirit, SSP Packer pride, whatever, we were there.

Young girls today have so many more options when it comes to sports that there are no longer enough girls interested in being cheerleaders. This is fine, but in my eyes cheerleaders will always fulfill a definite purpose. They help build spirit and excitement to motivate those around them to cheer their team on to victory. Cheerleaders keep on cheering until the very last second of the game. Cheerleaders never give up hope and—no matter the outcome—they will be there to support their team at the next game.

I was very hesitant to do a CaringBridge website. I felt it was a step toward surrendering and calling it quits. I wouldn't even go out and read CaringBridge pages when I was first diagnosed with breast canser in 2007. I chose to just send out update emails to let people know how I was doing while undergoing treatment then.

But when I was diagnosed with a recurrence earlier this year, one of my friends asked if I was going to do a blog or CaringBridge website. She said I was good at writing and updating with my emails. I thought about it and decided to do a CaringBridge site so that people would be updated about my treatment directly from me rather than the telephone game.

I never realized how important my CaringBridge site would become to me. It has been an essential tool in my healing, treatment and coping. It has been a great release for my thoughts and has lifted me up many times when I needed it. You see, you all have been my cheerleaders.

Some of you have been very vocal cheerleaders (like me), sharing your thoughts in CaringBridge guestbook entries, helping me stay positive and loudly never giving up hope. Some of you have been private cheerleaders, sending me offline messages of support, love, friendship and congratulations. Some of you are quiet cheerleaders. You may run into me out and about and mention that you read my CaringBridge, offer me encouragement and tell me I am in your prayers.

And some of you are anonymous cheerleaders, who I have not had the pleasure of meeting, but you continue to follow my progress and keep me in your prayers. Whatever kind of cheerleader you are, I am eternally grateful.

In addition to your cheering, you have covered me in prayers. The power of prayer has been proven. I remember reading in a sociology class at St. Thomas University that there is proven evidence people who are being prayed for recover, heal or survive better than people who are not being prayed for. I totally believe that. I believe in the power of prayer. I believe in positive thinking. And I believe that God heals and performs miracles today.

All of you have been essential in my healing and in my miracle. I believe I will be in remission for a long time from Stage 4 metastatic breast canser. (There, I said it, and we put it in its place.)

And it will be because of "my cheerleaders" that I was able to stay motivated, focused on the goal and filled with hope that we would be victorious!

God bless. Holding my head high and fighting like a cowgirl,
Sharyl

†

Sharyl,

I can probably say, like others, that I wish I had known you in high school. I can totally see you as a cheerleader. Your enthusiasm and positive energy are contagious. Most of the time, I get very emotional reading your journals. They really make me think that I do need to be more positive about my own life. You're such a great writer.

You are an inspiration to all of us out there, who wish we had been a cheerleader or who don't always think of the glass as being "half full." I am so happy that we are friends. I know you are a continual fighter and will always "fight like a cowgirl." I just love your spirit! I am always praying for you.

Love,
Sandy

†

Sharyl,

I just gotta quit reading these entries at work! Once a week, I read your newest entry and I cry! (Tears of joy, of course!) So glad to hear all is well!

Love ya,
Brenda

p.s. Since we are all your cheerleaders, where are our uniforms and, more importantly, what color are you making us wear???

God Will Lead Me to the Answer

Saturday, October 31, 2009

I had chemo yesterday. The infusion went well, but my arm and veins are a little sore today. Even though I drank 50 ounces of water before 11:45 a.m. (water is supposed to help bring out the veins), and they heated my arm up for about 15 minutes, my veins were still hiding on the nurse. She did get the needle in my trusty vein on the first try though.

I developed the flu the day after I received my awesome news, and I am now feeling the effects of a cold. My energy level is not 100%, but I was finally able to start exercising again this week, and that always helps to kick-start my energy and my attitude.

I saw my doctor on October 16th, before I started a new round of chemo the next day. All is going well with my body. As I mentioned, I have a couple of small left axillary (under the arm) lymph nodes that lit up on the PET scan—small enough that they probably won't show up on the CT scan I have on Thursday. Anything under a 2 is normal, and they measured 2.4.

The scan was taken just before I developed the flu. When I talked to the three different radiologists who tried to get samples after my PET scans lit up in October 2008, they each said PET scans can react for many different reasons, including colds and infections. My doctor has said that PET scans have an 18% false positive rate. Anyway, because those lymph nodes tested positive for canser in May, my doctor would like me to do another round of chemo in November and repeat the PET scan in December.

Depending on what that scan shows of the axillary lymph nodes, we will then determine a plan of treatment for the next few months, which may include staying on the trial, staying on two of the drugs, staying on one of the drugs or stopping chemo. I will have to pray on the decision, and I know God will lead me to the right answer.

Holding my head high and fighting like a cowgirl.

God Bless,
Sharyl

p.s. Brenda, the obvious choice for the color of the uniform is Pink. What else??? :-)

†

I am sooooo happy for you that things are looking up! That is wonderful! I knew that if anyone could beat this, you would. Keep doing all the things you're doing because they are working!

Big hugs,
Brenda

p.s. Okay, the cheerleader uniforms are pink. For you, I'll stomach it. What else are we to wear? I suppose saddle shoes. Pom-poms too? You are probably laughing at our awful uniforms. Bring it on!

On My Way to Being a Real Cowgirl

Monday, November 9, 2009

Wow! We have had some pretty spectacular weather in Minnesota during the last week. Over the weekend, I went out for a jog around the lake at our cabin. There are four little hills around the lake, and the last one is the longest. So many times as I was jogging, I thought "I should just walk," but while my head was saying it was okay to walk, it was as though my feet were not in agreement, and they kept running.

When I made it to the top of my fourth hill, I did the Rocky Balboa dance! (Only the deer and the squirrels saw me being so silly) I felt like I had just accomplished the New York City Marathon, because although I tolerate chemo well and I feel like a champ, the truth is that I don't have the strength, stamina or endurance that I did six months ago.

I was a tad disappointed in how long it took me to make my way around the lake. And while I wish I wasn't so slow, I am glad that I still have the energy to jog. I can still be hard on myself when it comes to exercise; Old habits die hard. But in challenging myself during exercise, I remind myself to stay focused on the goal, and the goal for me is long-term remission.

Yesterday, I was given a wonderful opportunity by my friend Sal. When I wrote about being a cowgirl, she told me about her brother and sister-in-law who have a ranch in Hastings, which is not too long of a drive from South St. Paul. Sal asked her brother and sister-in-law if I could celebrate remission by living out my dream of being a cowgirl.

Matt and Kelly invited me to their ranch and gave me the opportunity to ride Duchess, their daughter Brooke's horse. They have a beautiful piece of land and were very gracious to share their horses and their knowledge of horses with me and my kids. I think I am on my way to being a real cowgirl. Thanks, Matt and Kelly!

Kelly shared with me that the mother of one of her daughter's friends has been diagnosed with Stage 4 breast canser twice. When this woman had her initial diagnosis, it had already spread to her liver. They killed all the canser off, but unfortunately it came back again in her liver, and then she killed it off again and is again in remission. It fills me with so much hope and reassurance to hear about people surviving this yucky disease.

I think if you asked my doctor, she would not be ready to declare that I am in remission. I, on the other hand, am ready to declare myself in remission. She would tell you that the lymph nodes under my left arm concern her some, and I think she would also tend to believe that the chemo is keeping the canser from growing or spreading. I, on the other hand, believe the cancer is gone.

People can and do survive many stages of canser every day. People also die every day from canser and that fact does not escape me, but I am not going to live in fear of it. People also die from car crashes, heart attacks and crazy gunmen. We have no idea when our last day will be but we do know that we should enjoy every day that we are here, and I think there is validity to gratitude journals, positive thinking and the power of faith and hope.

However, I am ready to start feeling and looking more like me again. I would say I would like to be my old self again, but I think I have grown so much and gained so much insight that I don't want to go back, except to look like me while embracing the new me inside. Cosmetically, I am so ready for my eyelashes to come back! I really miss them the most. I bought a new wig the other day. I can't help myself from buying longer wigs. Some people might say, "You look nice with short hair. Why would you buy a long wig?"

Well, first of all, because I like long hair. Second, I probably won't grow my hair long again, so why not have fun with fake long hair while I can. And third, it initiates comments like this from my

Jacob: "Mom that wig looks pretty on you. You look like the old you, the one before canser." And, I have to admit, I liked the way I looked before I got canser.

I have faith that my doctor and I can come to an agreement to help me achieve balance in my recovery and continued treatment plan. If I stay on just the one chemo drug (still done intravenously), I think my lashes will grow back and the hair on my head will start to fill in. And the major side effect is high blood pressure, but since mine has not risen yet, I think I should be okay. I see my doctor on Thursday to go over my CT scan results from last week and then start another round of chemo on Friday.

Holding my head high and fighting like a cowgirl.

God bless,
Sharyl

My New Normal

Tuesday, November 17, 2009

Eeeeek!!!!! I should be used to this stuff by now. It should be my new normal. I think I handled it fairly well. Jason may say otherwise, but I don't think I was too much of a basket case.

Monday morning, bright and early, the nurse from my doctor's office called me and said, "Sharyl, your liver blood test that we took on Thursday was elevated. Can you come in and repeat the test today? Oh, and stop anything herbal, and no ibuprofen or Tylenol."

Hmmm, I developed a headache in the middle of the night and took an ibuprofen 600 and two Tylenol before I left for work this morning. Will this be a problem with the test then? But I said I would be in around 4 p.m.

A few minutes later, I saw my message light blinking. It was a message from the nurse again. "Do you think you can come in before 2:30 p.m. so that we can have the results by tomorrow morning?" Oh for heaven's sake, should I be worried? So I left work to go get the blood test done.

I was thinking about it throughout the afternoon and evening, wondering what could be wrong with my liver. And what could this mean for me? I really didn't have a bad feeling about it because I feel good, but I did ask my family if it looked like I had a tan.

This morning, the nurse called and said my numbers are still elevated but down significantly. My doctor said I would not have had time to do anything to make the numbers go down that much. I think it's good that they came down on their own. I have to repeat the blood test tomorrow so that my doctor will have the results Thursday morning to determine if I can receive chemo on Friday.

All of my other blood test results from last week were great. The white blood cells, platelets and hemoglobin were all good. My blood pressure is at 108/62. Hopefully my overworked liver will have filtered all the junk out by tomorrow morning so that I can make it work overtime again on Friday with chemo. My poor liver has worked very hard this last year.

I have had numerous scans in which they inject "stuff" that over time cannot be all that great for me. In addition, I've had a quick surgery to complete my reconstruction and remove a suspicious mole, a surgery to remove some female anatomy and about five attempted biopsies—not to mention a whole bunch of drugs. Sedation drugs for some of the biopsies, anesthesia for the surgeries, chemotherapy drugs, anti-nausea drugs (which include steroids, and we all know that long-time steroid use is no good for the liver), Tylenol, ibuprofen 600 (to wipe out my chemo headaches) and plain old, everyday toxins.

My doctor and I went over my CT scan last week, and there was no change from the previous scan. The scar on my liver still measures the same. That will most likely never change, and I can deal with that. Additionally, the lymph nodes don't show up on the CT scan. So the plan for the next two weeks is…(hopefully) chemo on Friday, a PET scan on November 30th and then I see my doctor on December 3rd to go over the PET results and make decisions about my treatment. I'm hoping and praying the PET scan is free of color so that there is no question about the status of my remission.

Holding my head high and fighting like a cowgirl.

God bless,
Sharyl

How Many Lives Need to Be Spared?

Friday, November 20, 2009

I'm glad to hear the government had to somewhat "retract" its position on the new guidelines it just issued for mammograms. I personally think it is a disgrace, and it is deeply disappointing that the government would negate the significant strides made in the advancement of breast-canser detection.

"They" say that there really has not been enough significant evidence that mammograms actually help detect breast canser early in women under the age of 50. In addition, "they" are saying there is no real benefit to self-exams either. My question is, "How many women's lives need to be spared for it to be 'enough'?"

Perhaps you should ask just one child whose mother's life was saved by a mammogram. Or maybe ask just one husband whose wife is here today because of a mammogram and find out if her life is "enough" proof to him to keep the guidelines in place.

I didn't find my lump by a mammogram, but I know there are many women under 50 whose lumps were discovered by a mammogram. Supposedly, someone like me with a family history would not have been denied an early mammogram, but who knows?

Genetic breast cansers only account for a small number of the breast canser population, so there are a lot of women out there getting breast canser without a family history. I would like to see mammograms started much earlier than 40, say for instance the late 20's, but no later than the age of 30.

"They" say that early mammograms can lead to too many unnecessary tests and biopsies, as well as anxiety. In my opinion, if you have to suffer through nervousness about a biopsy only to find out you don't have cancer, so be it. It beats the alternative—waiting 10 years to find out that you have canser that has spread throughout your body and that no amount of chemotherapy or radiation is going to help.

It is a lot more expensive to treat canser than it is to do a yearly mammogram and an "unnecessary" biopsy. Again, only my opinion, but it makes me wonder if "they" had an agenda and were not taking into consideration our wives, mothers, daughters, sisters, granddaughters, grandmothers, nieces, aunts and friends.

No chemo for me today. My liver blood tests are still elevated but continuing to go down. The biggest frustration in all of this is that I am a planner, and I hate messing with my schedule. I have stuff going on and chemo has its already scheduled place on my calendar. Ad-hoc rearranging of my calendar—huge pet peeve!!! But, I will get over it, and the best part is that I get to have a nice relaxing weekend free of drugs. No sleeping in, of course, because of that 8 a.m. hockey practice tomorrow. That's earlier than I go to work. Who schedules this stuff anyway? :-)

Holding my head high and fighting like a cowgirl,
Sharyl

Assumptions Are Not Fact

Thursday, December 3, 2009

The last couple of weeks have been quite a roller coaster for our family. My liver numbers were still elevated, so I wasn't able to receive chemo. And, I hadn't been able to kick the cold that had been hanging on for about five weeks.

On Friday, November 20th, I started using hair products to help stimulate the bald spots to grow. On Saturday night, when I was checking to see if there were any spots that needed product applied to them, I saw a bald spot on the back of my head, but more worrisome was the large swelling behind my left ear.

Immediately, I panicked. Jason was gone hunting, so I called my mom to ask if she would come take a look. We called the on-call doctor, and he didn't think it was canser, so I tried to relax and get some sleep. On Monday, I had to go to my oncologist's office for another blood test, and I asked the nurse to look at it. My doctor ordered a CT scan of my head, neck and soft tissue and sinuses.

I had the CT scan Tuesday evening. (I'm getting to know the evening CT staff very well.) It turns out that I had a huge sinus infection, which of course was a great relief. When you have had canser, there will always be a concern that anything and everything is canser. Who knew you could be so excited about an infection?

We went to Angelo's Pizza for dinner that evening and when I got home the nurse had left a message saying my liver numbers were elevated again. My doctor thought it could be from gallstones and wanted me to have an ultrasound. (My previous CT scan on November 5th showed gallstones.) So anyway, now I was kind of concerned about the gallstones. Over the weekend, I noticed that my skin was a yellow tone and my eyes were faintly yellow as well. In addition, I was very itchy, which is another symptom of jaundice.

I was scheduled for a PET scan on Monday, but called my doctor's office about my jaundice symptoms. They scheduled me for a CT scan of the chest, abdomen and pelvis on Monday afternoon. After the scan, I was told to wait and that I couldn't have the IV taken out until I heard from my doctor. She called me in the lobby and said my liver and gallbladder were both enlarged, and it looked like the bile duct was plugged. She said the good news was it didn't look to be canser-related—no new lesions or anything that would indicate canser.)

She wanted me admitted to the hospital for an upper endoscopy procedure. With the endoscopy, they would put a scope down the back of my throat and then go up into the bile duct to determine the cause of the blockage.

I decided against the hospital stay and said I would wait for her to call me to schedule it as an outpatient procedure. She instructed me not to eat anything in the morning in case I had to do the procedure the next day.

Tuesday they called me and said I needed to go back to the clinic for a blood test and then the GI doc would determine whether or not I needed to do the procedure that day. My liver-function numbers were elevated, so we had to head over to the hospital for the endoscopy procedure.

They give you sedation and pain medication intravenously during the procedure, but I was not sedated enough and could feel a lot of the pain. The doctor ended up having to put in a stent to allow the bile to flow. I heard him say something about canser. He told me he felt that there was a metastatic lesion on my liver putting pressure on the bile duct and causing the blockage. He told Jason the same thing. We were floored. He said he didn't see any canser but assumed that it was canser because I had canser.

I had two wonderful nurses assisting me that day, and I asked the one nurse what made the doctor think it was canser. I told him that I just had a CT scan the previous day and nothing showed up that would indicate canser. He said sometimes these things don't show up on scans. I was thoroughly confused and not convinced it was canser, but I obviously was devastated to hear such things.

And, I was in a lot of pain. Even so, they didn't send me home with any pain meds.

That evening, the pain was becoming unbearable so we called the GI clinic, and they sent in a prescription for Tylenol 3, which didn't do much. I normally have a pretty high pain threshold but this was severe. I called the doctor yesterday and said I was having significant pain, and he said, "Well that is to be expected. We made a cut at the top of the bile duct and whenever I would push on the stent, you would jump in pain." So, why didn't you give me a prescription when I left the hospital the day before??? I finally got some stronger pain meds, and they are helping to relieve the pain.

I talked to my doctor last night. She didn't know what was causing the blockage. She obviously cannot rule out canser but said she and the radiologist went over the scan results on Monday very thoroughly and didn't see anything to indicate canser. I will have a PET scan next week and pray the scan shows no color, which will mean that I am free from canser.

I think my body in the last six weeks has been under extreme pressure with gallstones, a virus and a sinus infection, and that this is more a result of that than new canser growth.

Thank you for your continued prayers and love.

Holding my head high and fighting like a cowgirl,
Sharyl

Signs of Hope

Monday, December 7, 2009

Last night when my kids and I did our dinner advent wreath, the devotion was Romans 5:2: *"And we rejoice in our sufferings, because we know sufferings produce perseverance, perseverance character and character hope and hope does not disappoint us."* Okay, first sign.

This morning while on my way to work, I realized I had forgotten my phone. I turned around to go back home to get it, and as I was getting off the highway I noticed part of a rainbow peeking through the clouds. Second sign.

I received some emails this morning from family offering much needed words of encouragement, and when I realized how many people are praying for me and offering their faith to me, it hit me: I have laid a solid foundation of faith for my healing, and I am so blessed to have so many of you offering to hold me up and fill in the cracks when I am feeling weak.

Jason told me in 2007 when I was first diagnosed with canser that this was just a bump in the road and I am a four-wheel drive truck, so I am shifting into gear. Yeehaw!

I have a PET scan today at 3:45 p.m., and I hope to report awesome news on Wednesday. God bless.

Holding my head high and fighting like a cowgirl,
Sharyl

†

Ant Sharyl,
I hope you feel good. I love you. I've been praying for you.

Hunter

Thank You for the Prayer Covering

Tuesday, December 8, 2009

My doctor just called and said my PET scan looks good. Everything looks the same or better since the last scan. I still have some lymph nodes lighting up, and she would like me to continue on the same treatment for a while longer. I will have a blood test tomorrow to make sure my liver functions are back to normal and that I can receive chemo on Friday.

I likely will be on the trial for a few more months and then switch to one drug. My doctor still doesn't have a great answer for why my bile duct was blocked. I truly feel my body was just working overtime to filter chemo drugs and fight off infections. This has been a huge wake-up call for me to give my body the rest it deserves when it is asking for it. It doesn't mean I will quit exercising, but I think I may take the winter off from jogging and do other types of exercise to keep it strong.

I will have to have the stent put in last week replaced with a more permanent type on either the 21st or the 22nd, but I told my doctor I would not allow the doctor who put it in to replace it. It's not that I am holding a grudge—I just won't allow someone who would instill unnecessary and unwarranted fear in me to be part of my care system.

Thank you so much for your prayers. I could feel the covering as my spirit was strengthened and restored. It was one of my most relaxing PET scans. I even got some Christmas shopping done while lying on the table!

God bless! Holding my head high and fighting like a cowgirl,
Shar

Christmas Blessings and People Rainbows

For God so loved the world, that He gave His only begotten Son, that whoever believes in Him should not perish, but have eternal life.
—John 3:16

Thursday, December 17, 2009

I'm wishing you all a very Merry Christmas and a joyous and blessed 2010!

The longer Jason and I are married, the more we seem to share the same brain. So many times we call each other with the same ideas or we just know what the other one is thinking.

The other night we had gone out to dinner with Jacob and Abby to celebrate my good-news PET scan and Jason said to me, "You know if there is something good to come out of you having canser, it is that you have met or connected with so many people that you otherwise may not have."

I had been thinking the exact same thing earlier that day. Now, I am not one of those people who calls canser a gift, or feels **glad** that I got canser because of how it changed my life for the better. But, I do think that the rainbows in life are appreciated much more after we experience some rain.

I have experienced lots of "people rainbows" during this rain. I've met people and made a couple of "pen pals" whom I may not have been blessed to connect with had I not had canser. I have reconnected with friends I haven't seen or talked to in a while, some even for many years, and what an awesome gift that is.

I've made friendships with people who would have otherwise just been acquaintances had they not reached out to our family during our time of rain. And I have deepened my existing relationships with my circle of family and friends. It stinks that it takes canser to make things like this happen, but it is what it is and like Dolly says, "If you want the rainbow, you gotta put up with the rain."

So many people have said, "How much can one family take?" Or, "You have had to deal with so much" and so on. I see how at times it could be viewed as though my husband and I have had a rough 10 years. But the absolute truth is that our family has a wonderful life. I am blessed to be loved by a good and honorable man.

Last night, he kept saying "Look at you; you're so cute." And I know he truly meant it. He really thinks his thin-haired wife with no eyelashes and eyebrows is cute. I think he's actually talking about more than just my physical appearance, and what an amazing gift that is for me.

We share in the joy of raising three beautiful kids. We were blessed to create a beautiful baby girl who we love so much and who also introduced us to people we would otherwise not have met and opened our eyes to seeing people beyond physical appearances (see above).

We have close, extended family and friends who make our lives richer by being a part of them. All in all, I would say Jason and I are abundantly blessed, and we are actually pretty lucky to know we can survive anything as long as we have each other, our kids and our support network of family and friends to help us through.

And I BELIEVE the power of prayer will keep that pesky canser from coming back to invade my body for a third time.

May God bless you all. Know that our family appreciates each and every one of you for how you have positively impacted our lives. As far as my treatment goes, I did receive chemo last week. I am no longer participating in the trial as I need to receive a port, which will make it easier to receive chemo and other drugs.

I'm down to two chemo drugs. (One still causes hair loss.) I will have chemo again tomorrow. I will take next week off and then get a port on December 28th and have chemo again on New Year's Eve and the following two Fridays.

These two drugs are given three weeks on, one week off., I will get a PET scan in late February and maybe in March go down to one drug. And then, hopefully at some point, I will take a long break from chemo, like forever...

Holding my head high and fighting like a cowgirl,
Sharyl

†

Sharyl,
You are so right. It is so important to count your blessings all around you every day! You are truly a blessing in my life as well! Happy Holidays to you, Jason and family!

Love,
Leanne

Each Scar Tells a Story

Friday, January 1, 2010

Happy 2010! I think this is going to be an amazing year, and I am filled with so much hope.

On Monday, I had a port put in my upper left chest. The surgery went well. I think I was pretty funny during the procedure and was babbling up a storm as I became less sedated. I don't think I even took a breath from the time they wheeled me out of surgery and back to recovery. All I got from the nurse was a couple of "hmmms." Then, I talked my mom's ear off until we got home. At one point in the surgery, I started humming.

Yesterday, I went for chemo and tested out my new port. They gave me a cream to numb the skin over the port an hour before I go in for a blood draw or chemo. The port is just under the skin. The area around it is still tender and swollen, so it caused some discomfort when the nurse cleaned the skin around it. But, when she inserted the needle for the blood draw, the port worked the way it was supposed to, so yay!!!

I picked up some of those trendy scarves and will be sporting that look for a while when wearing shirts with necklines that expose my lovely new scar. I did ask them before the surgery to make sure they didn't pop my breast implants—I had to go through a lot to get them. They reassured me they would stear clear of them, and they kept their promise. So now I will have another scar on my growing list of battle scars. Each one tells the story of a journey traveled and a promise of a hope for a brighter future.

I had to see the nurse practitioner before receiving chemo. My doctor is out on maternity leave, so I will be seeing a nurse practitioner for a couple months. My white blood cells were on the low side; the lowest since I started chemo. They were fine on Monday when I had the surgery, so I think it's just in response to the port placement. I don't intend to get excited about low white cells unless they don't rebound next week. And, even then, I won't freak because since I'm off the trial now, I can get a white-cell booster shot.

I only received one of the chemo drugs since the other can have bleeding side effects after a surgery. This is why I pulled off the trial; It had strict guidelines against chemo for six weeks before surgery. Non-trial patients only have to be off chemo for a week.

On a cosmetic high note, my eyelashes have started growing back. I'm not sure if it's because I had a three-week break from chemo or if they just started to grow again. If they fall out again, oh well, I will take what I have for now. And my hair is coming in nicely too, a little on the thin side, but I think my hair-growth stimulating products are working well.

Thank you for keeping me in your prayers and supporting our family. I mentioned a while back that one of my fears was having canser come back, and the other day I realized I don't have to be afraid of that anymore since it did come back, and I am surviving strong every day.

The medical community will not say that people with metastatic breast canser can be cured, but I do believe metastatic breast canser can be controlled and managed so that when there is a cure, we will be around to receive it. In the meantime, I am praising God for my blessings, healing and health. And I will always hold my head high and fight like the cowgirl that I am!!!

God bless,
Sharyl

Yogurt Does My Body Good

Friday, January 8, 2010

This could just be another one of "my theories" (I have many about lots of things—too many to get into), but this one I believe I have proven: Yogurt does my body good.

I hadn't been eating my daily yogurt over the holidays and didn't think it would be a big deal, but my neutrophils dropped to 1.2 last week; Normal is 1.3 to 6.0, so they were not drastically low but lower than they've been since I had the first of my two low weeks at the start of chemo. And I have been running between 3.0 to 6.0 all during chemo.

I think my numbers dropped due to a combination of the port surgery (invasion of the body) and lack of yogurt. From last Thursday through today, I put yogurt back into my diet, along with a few other power white-cell booster foods, and my neutrophils shot up to 4.4. Low neutrophils do not mean you are sick—just that your body doesn't have the same defenses to protect against germs, viruses and infections. So, I resumed my chemo schedule. And I tell ya, this port works pretty slick. The only weird thing is that I can taste the blood-thinner medicine, which is used to prevent clots, when they shoot it in my port before a blood draw and after chemo. But it gives me an excuse to have a Jolly Rancher.

Chemo again next week, and I have decided to lower the amount of the anti-nausea drug and see how I tolerate chemo and then probably take it out all together. I don't think I need it. The drugs I'm on don't have a lot of nausea side effects.

Holding my head high and fighting like a cowgirl,
Sharyl

I Am a COWGIRL

I Am a COWGIRL. I Am a Fighter. I Am a Survivor.

Therefore I tell you, whatever you ask for in prayer,
believe that you have received it, and it will be yours.
—Mark 11:24

Tuesday, January 12, 2010

This goes out to you T. I am always here for you, I love you with all my heart, and we will have more ups from here on out.

The other day, I came across the video Jason took of me ziplining in Colorado. The woman on the screen took me by surprise. I recognized her, but realized that I missed her. She had a sparkle and a fire, was full of energy and exuded confidence. She was full of joy and had an invincible attitude that emanated from the screen. Granted, she was doing something exciting and was full of adrenaline, but it was more than that. She was full of cowgirl spirit.

Late November and December of 2009 did a number on my cowgirl spirit. It was slowly being broken with each phone call of liver numbers, sinus infection, jaundice, blocked bile duct and an overzealous doctor telling me he assumed the worst. And, my free-flowing smile and laugh were not making appearances as often as they used to. I even said maybe I shouldn't jog anymore this winter, something that fuels me and keeps me in prime fighting spirit.

One day in early December, I decided to ask my doctor a question she had already given me the answer to six months earlier. I knew the answer would not be any different. Six months ago, when she gave me the news, I chose to live by my own set of numbers and manipulate the data to support a longer goal than what is normally statistically possible.

The woman on the video's attitude was "Take the numbers and shove 'em." The woman who asked the question in December decided to digest the answer and think "Okay, maybe 40, maybe 20, maybe 10 years is not realistic. Let's hope for five and anything after that will be icing on the cake." It's not that I'd given up on hope, faith or being positive. I just thought maybe I should be more realistic but keep hoping I would beat the statistics.

I'd also been having feelings of being "left behind." Over the last few weeks at the clinic, there have been a lot of people finishing chemotherapy, and there I sat in my chemo chair with no definite end in sight. I started to wonder if God had forgotten about my miracle. And sometimes I wasn't totally sure I believed what I was saying anymore—that I would survive this silly canser thing.

I had a battle in my head of trying to stay positive and faithful while the phone calls, blood tests, information and discouraging words were providing good opposition to believe otherwise. And although my PET scan showed great news, it is not "light-free," so my doctor is not quite ready to stop with my chemo yet.

But, I have slowly been returning to my cowgirl spirit and after watching that video, I decided I need to kick it into gear. I will be "that" woman again. For my family, for my friends and for me, I need to be her again. To remember that: I am a COWGIRL. I am a Fighter. I am a Survivor.

I miss the woman on the video, but now that I'm aware of it, I can bring her back. I'm here today for many reasons: because Jacob gave me a hug, because I have a very thorough doctor and, most importantly, because I have so many prayers lifting me up. I plan on doing everything I can to participate in all that life has in store for my family and me. And, I intend to share my wisdom, joy, grace, faith and confidence with my husband, children, grandchildren, friends and the world well in to my seventies and eighties.

Back in 2007, when I was out for a walk after digesting a bunch of canser information, the song "All Fired Up" by Pat Benatar came on. The song talks about learning from our mistakes and how challenges in our lives can be healed by faith. When it came on, I felt the need to run, and it birthed my love for jogging and my "invincible" attitude. (I know I am not invincible, but you need to feel that way when facing a life-threatening diagnosis.)

Holding my head high and fighting like a cowgirl,
Sharyl

†

Sharyl,

Your entry not only made me laugh, but cry. More importantly, it embraced for me how normal you truly are. It is to be expected that you will have highs and lows. Or that one day you will take the information from your doctor like a fighter and other days you will feel defeated and have to work that much harder to move into fighter mode!

And that is okay. I think when people are fighting/surviving cancer, we too often expect them to "keep that positive attitude," when in reality we just need to expect them to be true to how they feel and have good days and bad days like the rest of us.

Jen

Progression—The Mother of All Swear Words

Monday, January 25, 2010

I had a revelation the other day. I have been allowing myself to be imprisoned by the lack of an end date with chemo. People often ask me how much longer I have to continue with chemo, and the honest answer is that I have no idea. Before my doctor went out on maternity leave, I asked her if I could go down to just one drug at some point and her response was, "We'll see."

I thought, "Well that sounds like something I would say to my kids." I use that response when I kind of mean no but don't want to deal with an argument at the moment. Or as an incentive, such as, "If you keep your room clean, then 'we'll see,' *maybe* you can do or have what you're asking for."

So when people ask when I will be done with chemo, I kind of stumble nervously through an answer while I'm thinking, "If I am a good girl and have a good scan next time, I *might* be able to eliminate one drug." It was making me feel like a failure because from what I have read, the protocol is to continue on the drugs until "progression," or until the side effects become unmanageable.

For me, progression is a dirty word; The mother of all swear words in my life. But unlike the word recurrence was, it's not a daily, weekly or monthly thought in my mind. In fact, I rarely think of progression unless I'm reading something about chemo drugs. Ultimately, I think I will stop taking them when the doctors have realized I've been on them long enough that canser would have built up resistance to them. And, if canser hasn't progressed by then, it isn't going to.

But back to my revelation. I was talking to someone the other day who takes a medication for rheumatoid arthritis, and all of a sudden it hit me; What I am doing is no different than someone who is taking medication for rheumatoid arthritis, diabetes, liver disease or fibromyalgia, etc., to help manage a chronic condition.

I already knew canser could be considered a chronic condition, but it is the medication part that I was struggling with, mostly because of that whole hair loss thing. The major difference between the drugs I am taking and the drugs for the above conditions is the way they administer them. And, if you listen to the commercials, the list of side effects is about the same for those drugs as for the chemo drugs I'm on.

I had let myself get so wrapped up in thinking that the only way I can be considered "cured, healed, in remission" and so on is if I stop doing chemo. But that is not the case. Instead, right now, I am taking some preventive medications. The annoyance is that I have to go to the clinic and spend anywhere from an hour to an hour and a half to get them.

However, I now look at this like wearing a seat belt. I pray each time before I get in my vehicle that angels go before me to protect me and my family while we're in the car. But my angels (and that obnoxious dinging) also remind me to put on my seat belt before I pull out of the driveway, just in case someone else didn't command their angels to go before them.

I know I talk about this hair thing a lot but I promise I am not nearly as wrapped up in my looks as I used to be. The other day, I bought the *Crazy Sexy Cancer Survivor Guide* by my girl Kris Carr. It is more of an interactive journal and in the first chapter she made me aware that I actually really feel good about the way I look right now. It's a new confidence, a new "pretty" that encompasses so much more than my once lovely blond mane. It also helps that my brows and lashes are coming back, and they help to enhance my appearance. I wear a wig because it's cold outside, and I have very thin hair, and get fewer stares when I wear hair versus a bandana.

I'm really not any different than the majority of the female population who are not "true to their roots." And my hairdo requires a lot less maintenance, time and money than theirs, except for that wig addiction of mine.

I hope to be able to go wigless, hatless and bandanaless in the spring, but it all depends on that landing pad filling in on top of my head. Apparently, it isn't recommended to color your hair while on chemo. One of the nurses said, "You just never know what color you may get…" Yikes!

Holding my head high and fighting like a cowgirl,
Sharyl

Watch and Live

*Heal me, O Lord and I will be healed, save me and
I will be saved, for you are the one I praise.*
—Jeremiah 17:14

Thursday, February 4, 2010

Last week, I went to chemo armed with reading material. I had a copy of *Shape*, *Proverbs 31*, the first issue of the *Livestrong Quarterly* and the *Crazy Sexy Survivor Guide*.

I read through the first two magazines and then moved on to the *Livestrong* magazine. I was so excited when I saw an article about Kris Carr, my fellow cowgirl and author of *Crazy Sexy Survivor Guide* and *Crazy Sexy Cancer Tips*.

Kris is a quite a lady. Someday I hope to meet her. She is loaded with golden phrases and mindsets that help me reshape words, labels and ways of thinking. Although I do have a little difficulty fully adopting her eating habits. I know you can get protein through beans, nuts and tempah, but seriously that's a whole lot of beans and nuts, and have you tasted tempah? It tastes like cardboard.

And I think my husband would turn our lower garage into an outhouse if I kept that protein packing regimen. TMI, I know. So for me, it's easier to occasionally eat some turkey, fish or chicken. I suffer from a lot fewer headaches when I'm at full protein levels.

Anyway, as I was reading through the article about her, two phrases jumped out at me and made such an impact. For those of you who don't know much about Ms. Carr, she was diagnosed with a Stage 4 canser on Valentine's Day 2003. She had numerous lesions on her liver and in her lungs. The type of canser she has is extremely rare, and there are not a lot of treatment options. Today, she still has the lesions but they are not growing and some have decreased in size.

Kris has never had chemotherapy as it is not an option for the type of canser she has. She's had some treatments (I can't remember which), but mainly she's changed her eating and attitude. **Kris inspires me to be a cowgirl.**

Her doctor told her that they would watch and wait. But she decided she would "*WATCH AND LIVE.*" Those words flew off the page and hit me in the face. I think so many times when people are diagnosed with a life-threatening illness they hear those words, "Now we just watch and wait." And then what happens is we live in fear, and we wait, wait, wait. Wait for "it" to come back, wait for it to take over our bodies, wait for it to destroy us and our families.

I think we need to be vigilant about our health and treatment, but we certainly should not get in the mindset of waiting for something bad to happen. How could we possibly enjoy our lives waiting for something bad to happen?

In December, after the conversation with my doctor, I had been thinking about watching and waiting. I thought, I just have to wait, wait for the crap to hit the fan. Wait for canser to overtake my body. But seriously, who knows when that could happen? It could be six months, six years or it could be never. I am planning for the never option. So in the words of Kris Carr, I plan on watching my health and living!

Oh, and please don't call me sick. I hate that more than anything. I am not sick! I am in very good health actually. Sometimes, I get headaches or don't have as much energy or get a sinus infection. Or, for some strange reason, I have a blocked bile duct, but I am not sick. On the recommendation of medical counsel, I am treating my body with chemicals to prevent the progression of canser.

This brings me to the second golden nugget in our lives. We live so much by labels. In the medical community, I am labeled with Stage 4 metastatic breast canser. The medical community, at this present time, will tell a person they cannot cure metastatic breast canser. They can only offer treatment options and don't know how long canser can remain dormant in the body.

I disagree with this statement, and I think we can get caught up in the labels of staging, cure, remission, canser-free or whatever you want to call it. I mentioned in my last post that I don't think of progression very often, but Kris uses an excellent term to describe my status right now: "Progression-Free Remission."

Say it with me, "PROGRESSION-FREE REMISSION." As long as I don't have canser growing in my body and the medical community won't say that I am cured, I'm going with "PROGRESSION-FREE REMISSION." That works for me!!!

I will be having a PET scan on February 19th and am praying for awesome, wonderful, amazing results.

Holding my head high and fighting like a cowgirl,
Sharyl

†

Sharyl,
You are so positive and strong already! Now it can only be *WATCH AND LIVE!* Something we can all live by! You have been such a positive influence in my life, and you have given me support all along. Thank you so much!

Kelli

Doing the Rocky Balboa Dance Again

The weapons we fight with are not the weapons of the world.
On the contrary, they have divine powers to demolish strongholds.
—2 Corinthians 10:4

Thursday, February 18, 2010

I haven't been out for a jog since November when I ran around the lake at my cabin. If you remember, I said that there are four inclines around the lake, and as I made it up the last hill, I did the Rocky Balboa dance. I bumped into a friend after I made that comment and she said she liked picturing me doing that and said they do the same sometimes in her family for different victories.

I had been afraid to go out jogging for while. I was afraid that I wouldn't be able to do it. I came up with lots of excuses as to why I shouldn't go out and jog. Some of them were very legitimate reasons. It was too cold, there was too much snow. But my biggest obstacle was just plain old fear. What if I hurt myself? What if I caused my body harm? What if I simply couldn't do it anymore?

Theoretically, jogging is simple. You put one foot in front of the other, add a little speed and you are jogging. When I say I was afraid I couldn't do it, I really mean what if I couldn't go the distance I normally go? And what if I had to stop and walk?

I know what it would do to me if I had to walk. I would feel like I would be losing, losing the battle against canser. In my mind exercise allows me to feel some control over an out-of-control situation. Canser may have come into my body but I feel through exercise that I'm empowered to help kick it out and keep my body strong enough to tolerate the chemicals I put in it.

I had been doing moderate exercise at home during the prior weeks. Again, I was afraid to push myself to the normal exercising I had been doing prior to November because what if I couldn't do what I used to be able to do? What would that mean? Would that mean I'm losing the battle? But I began to believe in myself again, and I started doing some of my intensive exercise routines prior to my jog. I began to feel renewed, strengthened and empowered.

On that Saturday, I decided my poor pup needed some exercise. He's been going crazy wondering what he did that we don't go out and jog anymore. So, I put on my exercise pants and he started running in circles, probably thinking, "Is it true, are we going?" I started out walking with Blazer, using the excuse that it's best to ease into these things. Maybe I will listen to this song, then I will jog for the next, walk the next and so on. We made it about a block, looked at each other and said, 'This is for the birds, let's run."

I didn't have any expectations as to how long I would actually jog, and I told myself that I would be okay with having to stop and walk. As we continued to jog, I thought of what my friend had said to me about the Rocky Balboa dance and decided that when I got to my front steps, I would finish my jog with the Rocky Balboa dance again, but this time I added the punches!

Life is full of so many victories and should be celebrated as such. Unfortunately, I haven't been out for a jog since the 6th, but I continued my regular exercise routine last week. Over the weekend, after chemo, I developed a head cold and to use one of my husband's silly phrases, it "kinda knocked the stuffing right out of me." But I am feeling better and hopefully with all this snow melting will be able to resume a more regular outdoor jogging schedule. I know my dog would appreciate that.

Tomorrow I have my PET scan at 3:15, and I am expecting to do the Rocky Balboa dance to celebrate an even bigger victory with awesome news next week.

Holding my head and fighting like a cowgirl. Yeehaw!
Sharyl

†

Sharyl,

You continue to amaze me with your great fight against such a horrible disease. Thank you for all of the love and support you have given my mother, Rose, and our family. Your phone calls and letters have been uplifting for her. She looks to you as a source of support and a role model as she fights cancer.

God bless,
Jeff

Progression-Free Remission!

Saturday, February 27, 2010

I met with a doctor from my clinic yesterday. (My regular oncologist is still out on maternity leave.) The doctor started out by saying my blood work was great, but that my PET scan is not perfect. I responded, "It never has been..." He smiled at my humorous response and said there was a lymph node above my clavicle that lit up. I told him it lit up before, when I had a cold, and I had a doozy the week of my PET. He thought that would be a viable explanation, and it's also right next to my port line.

He did say that more importantly the liver and the lymph nodes under the arm are low-level lighting (dead tissue, i.e. scarring) and are stable, which to me is interpreted as Progression-Free Remission. He said that because the initial areas have remained stable, it is a positive indicator and that the new lymph-node lighting is most likely from the cold. Victory Dance!

Because he is not my regular doctor, and I don't think he consulted with my doctor before meeting with me, he was not going to change anything with my treatment protocol. I will continue chemo three weeks on, one week off for the eight weeks, with a PET scan at the end of the eight weeks.

I know with my whole heart that the next scan will show a complete healing and will show even more amazing results!!!

God bless and thank you again for the love, support and prayers received for me and my family. As always, holding my head high and fighting like a cowgirl.

Yeehaw!
Sharyl

How's That for Crazy and Amazing?

Monday, March 8, 2010

Another jogging story—my favorite kind next to good-news progress reports. After chemo, I sometimes like to do a little shopping as a treat to myself. While shopping on Friday, I ran into Jason's cousin Amy, who is a longtime runner and has participated in a *few* marathons over the years. We talked a little about running and how it makes us feel.

As I have explained before, I am not a marathoner. My jogs are usually only three to five miles long. But Amy and I talked about how there is something so true about a "runner's high." In my experience, I have found that jogging seems to produce just a slightly higher high for me than any other type of exercise, and she agreed it does this for her as well.

Up until about 2006, I hadn't been into jogging. I preferred hopping on the elliptical, doing an aerobics class, power walking or lifting weights. I had always been somewhat intimidated by running. It seemed like something for the most serious of athletes, especially those training for marathons. But once I tried it, I found running very empowering.

That same feeling can be achieved in all sorts of exercise—it's whatever makes you feel like you've pushed yourself just a little more or past your personal comfort level. When I was out for a walk that turned into a jog that day back in 2007, I felt that with every step I was crushing fear, negativity and canser into the pavement and so jogging for me is oh so uplifting!

Saturday afternoon, my doggie and I went out for a jog. The weather was beautiful. The terrain is still a little tricky though. I started out with gloves and a winter hat and about a mile into it, I took the gloves off and could have taken the hat off too but that bald spot may not have appreciated it… Or, more truthfully, I am not confident enough to expose my true looks.

Here comes another Rocky Balboa reference. Jacob downloaded the "Eye of the Tiger," and I thought it would be a good running song so I downloaded it as well. True story. As I turned the corner to run up the hill to my house, I measured it up and thought, "I will jog as long as I can and if I have to stop, we will just walk the rest of the way."

As I started trekking up the hill, the "Eye of the Tiger" started streaming through my ears. And as the words about survival rang in my ears, I pictured myself as Rocky in the scene of the movie, where this song is playing and he is running up the hill in the snow.

So when I reached the top of the hill, Blazer and I celebrated. I raised my arms, jumped around and said "We did it! We made it!" I am sure the woman in her driveway shoveling ice thought I was nuts, but, oh well; I am proudly just a cowgirl with a will to survive.

Yesterday evening I was at Trader Joe's, and the quirky checkout dude said, "Okay, tell me something crazy and amazing about your weekend." I was kind of tired and not feeling very quick-witted, so I babbled something about my kids' hockey games. As I was driving home, I wanted to go back and change my answer. I wish I would have said, "Well, I had my weekly chemo on Friday afternoon and then took my dog out for a three-and-a-half mile jog on Saturday afternoon. How's that for crazy and amazing???"

It's really not that much of either, but I'm hoping to change what people see when they see someone who has been labeled with canser. To demonstrate that people living with and/or being treated for canser can live super productive, fulfilling and healthy lives. And, that we have crazy, amazing wills to SURVIVE! Coincidentally—or maybe not—the group Survivor sings "Eye of the Tiger." Hmmm, these things can no longer be ignored.

Holding my head high and fighting like a cowgirl,
Sharyl

†

Well, I think you are kind of crazy and definitely amazing! Always have been, always will be! Giddy up, cowgirl!

Love,
April

†

Sharyl,
I wonder if you know how inspirational you are. After you talked about running after chemotherapy, I was out running, and thought if I can't make it up this hill (big one by my house) being perfectly healthy then I never have a reason to complain.

When you said you wanted to go back and have a do-over to the clerk at Trader Joe's, I though you did get a do over here in this online entry.

I think about you quite a lot and wish for you a total and complete healing here on earth. Your faith is really amazing. When I go through struggles, I have a hard time turning things over to God and trusting that he will make it okay. With you, it seems so effortless.

I hope you and your family have a great Easter,
Barb

My Butterfly Story

Friday, March 19, 2010

For those of you who know my family and me, you likely know that butterflies are very special to us. For the last 10 years, we have taken much joy in seeing butterflies. We have butterflies all over our house and cabin, and we put up a Christmas tree every holiday season that is adorned with angel and butterfly ornaments.

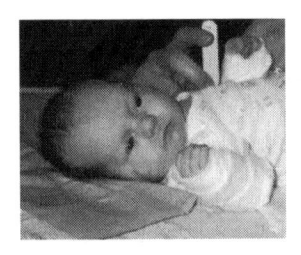

One of the reasons butterflies are so special to us is that when our daughter Caylin was born, she was diagnosed with a rare skin condition called epidermolysis bullosa (EB). Children with EB are called "Butterfly Children" because EB is described as a skin condition in which the skin is so fragile, it is like butterfly wings.

But butterflies also represent the soul, faith, beauty, transformation and hope. I found a beautiful explanation on the "whatsyour-sign/butterfly-animal-symbolism" website. Here's what it said:

"The butterfly unquestioningly embraces the changes of her environment and her body. This unwavering acceptance of her metamorphosis is also symbolic of faith. The butterfly beckons us to keep our faith as we undergo transitions in our lives. She understands that our toiling, fretting and anger are useless against the turning tides of nature—she asks us to recognize the same. We are all on a long journey of the soul.

"On this journey, we encounter endless turns, shifts and conditions that cause us to morph into ever-finer beings. At our souljourney's end, we are inevitably changed, not at all the same as when we started on the path. We look again to the grace and eloquence of the butterfly and realize that our journey is our only guarantee. Our responsibility is to make our way in faith, accept the change that comes, and emerge from our transitions as brilliantly as the butterfly." WOW!!!

After our sweet Caylin passed away, we took much comfort in butterfly sightings. The day Jason showed me the property where we would build our cabin, we were greeted by a little butterfly that fluttered around us and even seemed to be leading us around the lot. The butterfly stayed with us the entire time as if to show us our "happy place" where our family would make beautiful memories.

One glorious April morning about nine years ago—April 24, 2001 to be exact—the sun was shining brightly, and the weather was warm. I received a phone call from a doctor in Philly who had been working on identifying whether the amniotic sample from the baby inside me contained the genetic mutations Jason and I carry for EB. The baby did not have my genetic mutation, which meant that worst-case scenario the baby would be a carrier (like Jason and me) of EB but would not be affected by EB.

I was so excited and couldn't wait to call Jason with the news but he was at work and out on a fire run. And then for each person I called after him, I got no answer, just voicemail. I was overjoyed with the news but couldn't reach anyone to share it. I worked pretty close to home, so I decided to go home for lunch to reflect.

When I got home, I stepped out on my deck to enjoy the warm sun and rested my arm on the railing. I looked down, and the teeniest, tiniest butterfly landed next to me. I stood very still, and the butterfly hopped up on my finger. She stayed there for a few seconds, then hopped off of my finger and onto the railing, made a couple more jumps and flew away. I believe with every fiber of my being that butterfly was sent by Caylin. She knew I needed someone to share the news with so she sent a little butterfly to me, as if she were saying to me, "See Momma, everything is going to be alright. Now smile and be happy."

As I was thinking about sharing this story, I wasn't exactly sure how I would close the post. I thought that since I haven't seen a real butterfly for over six months, I didn't have a way to tie it all together. Since this post was supposed to be in April and I may or may not have had a visit from a butterfly, I thought that I could say something like this, "Although I haven't seen a butterfly yet, I know my little Caylin will send another butterfly my way as a little gift to me and as a reminder that she again would tell me, 'See Momma, everything is going to be alright. Now smile and be happy.'" And then I would share that my scans showed no canser.

Last night, a friend stopped by with a gift that made her think of me. We talked for a few minutes and after she left I unwrapped the gift and what fell into my hands took my breath away: A pewter butterfly ornament with the inscription *"For With God, All Things Are Possible."* I guess my little angel didn't want me to have to wait until April when the butterflies return to send me a message.

As I looked to my kitchen window and surrounding shelves, I saw other butterfly gifts that had been given to me recently: The porcelain ornament from my mom, the glass ornament from my aunt, the music box from my mother-in-law and the rock from my sister-in-law. Each was given to me as an expression of their love for me and to symbolize hope, miracles and strength as I have embraced the transformation a canser diagnosis has brought to my life!

Whatever struggle you may be going through, please know God will provide you with the strength, faith and hope to endure, embrace and grow from your challenges, heartaches or disappointments. He will send people, trinkets and songs but most importantly His Word to remind us of His everlasting love and care.

We are each asked to be vessels to share and spread God's love. And, as my friend and I discussed last night when I called to thank her for the butterfly, if God nudges you to share His loving kindness, don't ignore the nudge because your act of kindness may prove to be a precious gift delivered at the most perfect time. Now smile and be happy.

Holding my head high and fighting like a cowgirl,
Sharyl

†

Sharyl,
Thanks so much for sharing this. As another "butterfly mom," I truly appreciate your pulling happiness and joy out of your pain.

Praying for you,
Laurie

†

Sharyl,
What an amazing gift you have. The thoughts you share here on your CaringBridge site should be made into a book. You have made me laugh, made me cry and made me believe that miracles do happen. I will never, ever look at a butterfly the same way again!

What a beautiful, beautiful story. I believe with all my heart that your sweet, little, baby girl is truly sending you those butterflies. I also believe that those little butterflies could be God sending you your little girl when you need her the most.

It's almost spring and soon the butterflies will be out in full force, and the good news of your scan will follow. May your heart always be full of butterflies and may you realize the power you have to reach people with your words. Sometimes we never understand why God gives us crosses to bear, but I have to believe He knew that you would take this experience and touch people in a way that is very special!

I will continue to pray for you and your family, especially your sweet, little butterfly!

Mary

Optimism Is Good

Then Jesus said to her, "Woman, you have great faith! Your request is granted."
—Matthew 15:28

Tuesday, March 30, 2010

Last week, I had to have my biliary stent replaced. This was the stent that was put in my bile duct in December to open it as result of an enlarged gallbladder and liver.

The doctor who originally put the stent in said, "I should probably put in a permanent stent, which means it could never come out, and it can get clogged, which I'm guessing could lead to more blockages." Not really the solution I was looking for... This doctor also told me I had a canserous lesion on my liver causing the blockage, which proved to be FALSE.

That December day was one of the most devastating days of my life, next to the day a doctor delivered the terrible news two days after our daughter was born that she had a "lethal," unpronounceable disease for which there is no cure, handed us a three-page article written circa 1983 and walked out, leaving us staring at each other and wondering what the heck he had just said. There are some stinkers in the medical field, but on the flip side, I believe there are more gems out there than bad bedside apples.

The stent put in this December is designed to last only a couple of months. I had it replaced in late January, but had a different doctor replace it. I had an encounter with the doctor I selected for the procedure back in November of 2008 when he tried to get a look at one of my lymph nodes that was lighting up on a PET scan. He has a very calming bedside manner and put me at ease.

At the hospital on Wednesday, I was concerned because his notes from January said that we may want to discuss the permanent stent. When I got to the procedure room, he said he wasn't ready to put in a permanent stent yet. He thought we should see how things are going and also discuss everything with my oncologist. He got me nice and relaxed and very sleepy so that I wouldn't feel the tube going down my throat and the stent being replaced.

When I woke up and became a little less groggy, the doctor came to me with a big smile on his face and said, "Well, the opening is less narrow." Being that I was still foggy, I couldn't for the life of me figure out what "less narrow" meant. Was that good or bad? By the smile on his face, I determined it was good. He said he was going to be optimistic and that when I come back in May, the stents will have done their jobs and can come out for good.

I started another round of chemo last Friday. I'd been having some pain in my left arm over the last few weeks, and the nurse practitioner thinks I may have lymphedema in that arm. It's kind of weird since supposedly if I was going to get lymphedema, it should have been in my right arm—the side from which I had lymph nodes removed in 2007. But the recurrence of canser showed up in lymph nodes on the left side, and my port was put in on the left side, which is when some of this discomfort started, so it could be a result of the port surgery. I did have some lighting of the lymph nodes under my arm on my last PET scan, but the radiologist didn't think it was progression; He thought it was inflammatory.

So, I'm going to keep the faith and continue believing that I'm healed and, as always, hold my head high and fight like a cowgirl.

Sharyl

p.s. On Wednesday, a friend picked my kids up from school, since I couldn't drive. She brought them back to her house for a little while. Now, I thought seeing butterflies in late April was kind of early, but Jacob and his friend caught two butterflies that day.

p.p.s. Thanks, Rosie, for the butterfly hat. I love it. It matches my eyes.

My Secret Weapons—FAITH, HOPE and LOVE

Wednesday, March 31, 2010

I've been struggling a lot over the last few days, and my emotions and thoughts have been running wild. It could be attributed to a lot of things: The upcoming 10-year anniversary of our Caylin's passing, the three-year mark of when this canser mess started for me, the one-year mark of this recurrence nonsense and just plain old, I have had enough of this canser crap!

I shared some of my fears and frustrations with my mom and asked her, "Am I being ridiculous with all my talk about hope, faith and healing?" Because in all honesty, sometimes God's answer is to not heal our physical infirmities. And what if I'm just fooling myself? What if God's decision is to not heal my body? Will I then look foolish for being so hopeful?

I don't have what a lot of people would consider "big" dreams. Sure, I have things I wish I would have done or that I think would be nice to do. Like I wish I would have gone to school for fitness versus accounting and fulfilled my dream of opening a fitness center. Would I like to share my story with the world in a best-selling book? Heck yeah. Or if I had the opportunity, would I like to travel the world? Of course. But my true dreams are much simpler. All I really want is to grow old with my husband.

And, if I nevier set foot farther than Wisconsin in the next 40 years, but got to spend those years waking up next to Jason and watching our children grow into loving, God-fearing, responsible adults, I would consider it a very full life. As long as I got to witness my children's graduations, weddings, the births of their children and all the little moments in between that add up to a pretty great life, I would die happy and fulfilled.

I know that life is full of ups and downs, but I was having a bit of a pity party; I'd just like to spend some time on the upside instead of so much time climbing to pull myself out of the pit.

Music is a huge part of my life, and I take a lot of comfort in finding songs that lift my spirit and soul. My brother and oldest son will probably cringe at this one, but I thought of Miley Cirus' song "The Climb" after I mentioned my feelings to my mom. When that song comes on while I'm out jogging, I seem to jog a little faster, hold my head a little bit higher, and my faith gets a little bit stronger. This may be the reason I feel the need to celebrate when I jog up a hill; it's like my life.

Sometimes I need to remind myself that tomorrow isn't promised to any of us. And while I'm living out today, I need to remember that whether I'm standing at the bottom of the mountain trying to figure how to tackle it, in the midst of climbing it or standing at the top of it rejoicing, the faith and hope I live by will be with me at every stage in my journey. And I need to remember that my life is so full of the love I dream of. It's not foolish to be filled be with faith and hope, and I do believe God will honor my request to live a long, full life of awesome, every-day moments.

I will be here to witness Jacob's hockey team bring a state title to South St. Paul in the year 2020 :-), to see what becomes of Taylor's musical talents, to see whether my daughter decides to be a dancer, hockey player or something else altogether in high school. To share in their dreams as they start families and careers of their own. To hold my husband's hand each day, and share those moments with him, all the while reminding ourselves that no matter where we are in the ups and downs of life, each day we share life together, we can say *"Our cup runneth over"* with joy and blessings.

In all honesty, I feel pretty awesome. I have a little discomfort in my arm. I have annoying chronic sinus congestion. But do these things impede my life? Absolutely not. For the most part, I'm able to do everything I was doing a year ago.

Almost every person has been touched by canser in some way in their life, and it is true that CANCER SUCKS. I **try** not to get stuck on the idea that I should have been like the millions of other breast canser survivors who haven't had to face recurrence. For whatever reason, that nasty canser came back to try and wreak havoc on my body. It's good then that I have my secret weapons in FAITH, HOPE AND LOVE.

Thank you for supporting me in renewing and strengthening my faith. Thank you for your posts, emails, cards and phone calls in which you share your faith, prayers and stories with me. I feel honored to be a part of them. I hope you all have a blessed Holy Week and Easter Weekend. I pray that the miracle of the Resurrection of Jesus provides a miracle to transpire in your life as we thank God for sending His son to die for our sins, sickness and transgressions.

God bless,
Sharyl

†

Sharyl,
Suffering can do one of two things: it can make us feel hopeless or it can give us hope. It is how we choose to embrace the suffering that determines how we respond. We can either: dwell on the suffering and become angry, desperate people, or we can look to God for strength and comfort. Those who choose to trust in God in turn build character and indeed HOPE.

You ask if you are being foolish with all of your talk of hope. I say NEVER. Hope is never foolish. It's what keeps us going. It's that small light in the darkness that helps you find your way. Hope is contagious. Your HOPE gives others HOPE. When those moments of doubt creep in, talk them through with someone or write about them and pretty soon HOPE will again triumph.

Always remain HOPEFUL.

I Love You,
Mom

†

Sharyl,

The thoughts and fears you shared today were wonderful. Powerful enough to make me stop, think, respect and be thankful for what I have. Not what I don't have, haven't been or haven't done, yet. Thank you very much, for saying it just the way you felt it.

Many of us move through the years as friends, parents/partners, etc., and we think, reflect, wish: "If only I had done this, said this, started this, not done this." Then we wonder, "Would it really have been better, worse, more rewarding, had a better/worse outcome?"

In reality it doesn't matter, does it? We have what we have and should cherish and take the time to really enjoy it. We need to thank those who've shared in those things we have been privileged to enjoy and learn from. These marvelous things have shaped us, helped create the paths we were meant to live. We all just take different signs, times to enjoy, be thankful for and share how lucky we've been to be blessed. It seems we somehow get stuck on the sadness or "thought cycle" instead of just being happy about what we do have, had or will have.

It's really simple, isn't it? Be happy, grateful and thankful and move forward to the best of our abilities. Enjoy each day for what we've learned. Try to make the next day better than the day before. And always share because there is somebody out there who will benefit from your experience. It makes it seem so much easier to me after reading your post that being happy, thankful and grateful is all I need. And, it reminds me to spread good thoughts to everyone I meet each day.

Thanks for your thoughts and inspiring words!
Linda

Cowgirls Dust Themselves Off

Canser Is a Jerk

Tuesday, April 13, 2010

Last week at chemo, I had a friend with me. It was nice to have her company. Normally when I go, I bring a book to read, joke around with the nurses, occasionally make conversation with the other patients, but mostly I just get my drugs and go shopping (hee-hee).

My friend sat down, and we immediately started chit-chatting about the silly event planning conversations between eight-year olds, Little League drama and the Bon Jovi concert she attended the night before. Our conversation was relaxing and fun, and we laughed and smiled a lot.

Occasionally, I would glance over at this young woman and her family in the corner, and I could tell I was becoming a source of frustration for them. But I was having such a nice time with my friend, and I just want to be happy because even though I am surrounded by canser every day, I just wanted to talk about other stuff with my friend. Finally, the young woman's mother walked over and said, "Can I ask you a question? My daughter wants to know how you can be in such a good mood."

For a brief moment, I felt guilty. I felt as though I should be quiet, and I should stop being so insensitive to the people around me. After all, this is canser and it's no laughing matter. I started talking to her mom, and I explained to her that I had a recurrence with canser, and I've been doing chemo for almost a year now and this is my life.

As I talked more with her, her daughter and husband, the young woman shared some of her emotions, fears and concerns about this whole canser mess, and the following thought came to mind, "Canser is a jerk." (My husband hates that word, so it's a good word to describe canser.)

Canser is ugly and mean and needs to be eradicated. It concerns me that it does seem to be affecting more and more "younger" people. I think "younger" is defined as 40 to 50 by the medical community. Since my diagnosis in 2007, I know a lot more people under the age of 50 who've been diagnosed with canser than those over the age of 50. And, a lot of these people lead very healthy lives; People who are in the "prime" of their lives and now have to add a whole new set of stressors to the already normal daily stress that we all live with.

But what frustrates me most about canser is that it can steal people's smiles and laughter. And I love to see people smile and laugh, rising above the "jerks" of the world. As we all know, laughter can be contagious, and the giggles are something I love to catch.

I will keep on living my life, going about my everyday responsibilities and talking about what everybody else talks about: kids, jobs, family, friends, future dreams and plans and, of course, Little League drama. And very soon, I will put that whole canser stress in the past where it belongs. I'll also remind myself and my fellow survivors that we need to keep laughing and smiling as to not let that jerk, canser, get the best of us.

I'm having a PET scan Thursday at 7:45 a.m. I'm really looking forward to the results and the great news that will be revealed. On February 23, 2010, I had the experience of having another Holy Spirit healing (similar to the Anointing of the Sick sacrament I received in June). This was after I had a PET scan and was awaiting the results. I was asked by my cousin's husband if he, along with others, could pray for me.

They began to pray for me, and as they laid their hands over me, I could feel the Holy Spirit moving through me. I experienced feelings in which I could feel the ugliness of canser, afflictions and sin being released from my body. I stand firm that this scan will show, without a doubt that I am in remission.

I again thank you for all your prayers, love and support. If some of you have been praying specifically for my arm, it has been helping. The strain that I had been feeling before is gone. Unfortunately, my fingers have now been experiencing some neuropathy. A year of chemo will do that to you, I guess. It's getting uncomfortable to text on my Blackberry. I may have to go old school and actually call people. Fortunately, I still have the gift of gab.

Smile and laugh often! Holding my head high and fighting like a cowgirl,
Sharyl

p.s. Thanks, Rosie. I put my cowgirl magnet on my fridge to remind me every day to say a little "Yeehaw" before I go on my way!

†

> *"And we rejoice in the hope of the glory of God. Not only so, but we also rejoice in our sufferings, because we know that suffering produces perseverance, perseverance character and character hope. And hope does not disappoint us, because God has poured out His love into our hearts by the Holy Spirit, whom He has given us."*
> —Romans 5:2-5

Love You, Bear! Keep fighting like a cowgirl!
Marie

Sunday Is Coming

Wednesday, April 21, 2010

A few weeks back, after I posted about climbing a mountain and such, I had watched an episode of Joel Osteen that was titled "Enjoying your Life." Joel started out talking about climbing a mountain and explained that we actually have very few mountain tops and more climbs. He defined mountain tops as events like weddings and graduations, achieving goals, as well as being healed and pulled out of our pains and pits. I didn't actually get to finish watching the message until just last week.

After my PET scan, I got sucked into a mini-depression. My mind was racing with negative thoughts and fears. I get very anxious when I have to take my tests. It's something that I've been struggling with ever since this junk started. I don't do well with the anticipation and waiting. The tests themselves are no big deal. It's the "what-if monster" that can get the best of me.

Anyway, last week I reached out to my cousin, who prayed for me via email. I could feel the power of the prayer wash over me and put a mental block on my fears and negative thoughts. She suggested I find some quiet time that day to spend in prayer and thought. That afternoon after work, I was mentally exhausted and drained. So, I rested on my couch and remembered that I had a couple of Joel Osteen messages on TIVO. I finished watching the episode about enjoying my life. The next message was titled, "Sunday is Coming." It was the message for Easter weekend.

Joel started by saying that although it may feel like a Friday, the darkest day in the Christian calendar, Sunday, is coming. He got my attention because I thought I am in a Friday right now, and I am so ready for my Sunday. Joel went on to say, that when Jesus died on the cross, he declared, "It is finished." I am declaring that canser is finished in my life.

Joel explained that we need to stay confident in the hopes, dreams and prayers we have requested from God. It may take longer than we expect or hope to see our prayers come to fruition, but if God puts something in our hearts, He will always see it to completion. And, as I learned in one of my devotional books, *"Delays are not denials."*

Joel further explained that as we all know, God answers prayers in His time, not our time, and that even though we are ready for it to be Sunday, someone else who is to benefit from our Sunday may not be ready yet. Interesting!

I met with my doctor this morning to go over the results of my scan. A couple of the lymph nodes that lit up on the last scan, were gone (like the one above the clavicle) but a few different ones are lighting up. However, neither my doctor nor I are concerned about them because of my history with lymph node lighting. My original liver lesion showed a slight uptake in coloring, and I have a new spot on my liver that shows low-level lighting.

What she wasn't able to tell me was if this new spot was actually one of the other lesions I have on my liver that showed up in the past, but didn't express any reaction on the PET scan. Either way, she wasn't terribly concerned. The original spot on my liver showed a lighting on the scan a year ago, three times darker than the spots now showing up on the scan. My doctor said she doesn't consider this progression, so I am going with Kris Carr's term and again calling this Progression-Free Remission.

I continue to stand firm that this is all leading up to a revealing scan of healing. PETs are extremely sensitive tools for measuring canser. And, as one of my interim doctors told me, the great thing about PETs is they don't miss canser, but they can sometimes misread something as canser. I think my body is still flushing junk out of my system, and I know I am healed.

My doctor also ordered a tumor marker test that helps determine if canser has come back or is progressing. Well, my blood tests have always been in the normal range but have been gradually increasing over the last year. Normal is anything under 36 or 34. My last tumor marker test in February was at 36. The most recent blood test a couple of weeks ago showed that my tumor marker number had gone down to 24!!! It stands to reason that if canser were progressing in my body, the number would not go down!!!

The disappointing news for me is that I need to continue on the same chemotherapy regime. So, I will have chemo again this Friday. I will do two more cycles and then have another scan. I started doing yoga at home, and it helps with the strain I get under my arm at times. I also believe it helps to release the nasty toxins from my body. I'm able to do pretty much everything I was able to do last year, except I've had to modify my exercising, which is a pretty big thing for me.

I'm very competitive with myself when it comes to exercise and to have gone from a seven-minute, 30-second mile to a sometimes 12-minute plus mile is disappointing. However, it has now become not how fast or how long I can run, but that I still can and it feels victorious every time I do.

As much as I look forward to putting chemo in the past, and as much as I miss my eyelashes and full head of hair, I believe I'm making the best decision to continue on this course of treatment and to prepare for my Sunday. I will always declare that I have a pretty awesome life. I'm abundantly blessed and God is Good!

One more thing, I watched a webinar a few months back given by a doctor at the Cancer Centers of America and basically what I got out of it is that for every day, every month and every year we live, we are that much closer to new treatments and one day closer to eradicating this stupid disease! PRAISE GOD and AMEN!

Holding my head high and fighting like a cowgirl.

God bless,
Sharyl

†

Sharyl,

You inspire me. I read your entries and each one is so full of hope and determination. You take all who read your journal through a journey of what could be looked at as despair and hopelessness down the path to God's grace and love.

You are blessed, Sharyl, to have the ability to go through the pain and upset of your cancer and write about the peace and tranquility you find each day.

You words are always a lesson to me. When I feel that the day that I'm having is not the best, I think about you and my attitude is put back into perspective. I want to thank you for that.

May God continue to bless you,
Deb

When I Look Back

Being confident of this, that He who began a good work in you will carry it on to completion until the day of Christ Jesus.
—Philippians 1:6

Tuesday, May 11, 2010

I am officially a three-year Survivor. Yay, me!!! It is amazing how much happens in the span of three years. Three years ago, I woke up from a surgery and a nurse gave me the great news that canser had not spread to my lymph nodes.

The next day, I attended the South St. Paul Educational Foundation Dinner, where over $100,000 in scholarships were awarded to South St. Paul High School Seniors.

I wasn't sure if I should go to the dinner since I had just had a major surgery, but this was a pretty big day in Taylor's senior year. The kids don't know which scholarship they will be awarded until the night of the dinner, but in my opinion, regardless of the amount, it is quite an honor to win any scholarship from this organization. Because of a "connection" I have, I was strongly encouraged to attend the banquet and told that I wouldn't be disappointed in Taylor's award.

The truth was that I wouldn't have missed it for the world. My darling son wore a pink tie in my honor, and Jason, Taylor and I went to the banquet. When I scanned through the program at all the different awards, I knew which Taylor had won before they called his name.

When I attended Jefferson Elementary, there was a tiny woman who was an assistant principal. She had the loudest voice you could imagine. Although her voice was intimidating to a young child, she had a smile and laugh that instantly put you at ease. As an adult, I would see her at church, and her voice never faded. She truly lit up a room and made her presence known. Always gracious and kind, she was one of those teachers who remembered your name, your siblings' names and your parents' names. What a gift!

This tiny little woman with the booming voice was Mary Jane Morin, and my son won a $1,000 scholarship in her memory. Taylor received the scholarship because his educational plans include pursuing a degree in education in order to make a difference and have an impact on the lives of children, like so many teachers do. I don't know a lot about Mary Jane's battle, but I do know she had breast canser, and it filled me with great pride that Taylor received an award in memory of such a wonderful lady.

In the three years since my diagnosis, Taylor graduated from high school, Abby participated in her very first dance recital dressed as a little sunflower and Jacob started kindergarten. Abby started kindergarten the following year. Jason got a job on the fire department's rescue squad, Taylor finished his degree at Inver Hills Community College and transferred to the University of Wisconsin at River Falls. My parents celebrated their 50th wedding anniversary, Jason and I celebrated our 10th wedding anniversary, Jacob just made his first communion a week ago, and it's almost summer vacation again. Look out cabin, here we come.

We've had some bumps along the way these last three years, mainly just that annoying recurrence last year and a couple other medical mishaps, but mainly they have been filled with every-day blessings and love in the same way your lives have been filled with blessings and love.

In the three years since my initial diagnosis, I have lost some body parts, gained some back, lost my hair twice and have struggled with my reflection in the mirror. I don't have to shave my legs or underarms very often (or pluck my chin hairs) which is not so bad, but painting my face to make it appear as though I have eyebrows and eyelashes and covering my head gets a bit old after a while.

Like a lot of people, I am my own worst critic. The other day, I thought to myself, "I feel bad for my kids because they have to look at me and I am not so attractive." I wondered if other kids say things about me to them about how I am not so pretty without a wig, and ask why I sometimes wear hair and other times not?

Then, I read something in my *Crazy Sexy Cancer Survivor Guide* about a woman who lost her hair to chemo and a child asked the woman's son how he could deal with his mom not being pretty. He said, "You are just not looking at my mom where it counts, otherwise you would see how prettiful she is." I was reminded that my kids and husband tell me all the time how pretty I am. They don't see what I see in the mirror, and I bet they would defend me in the same way if someone said I wasn't very nice looking.

After I learned I would continue on chemo, I was sad that I was still going to be hairless, and I whined and cried to a friend. This was her response. "While you may look different to yourself, there is so much of you that looks the same to us. Your cheekbones still stick out, making for a beautiful face shape, your coloring is the same, your baby blues still sparkle and your lips are still full. There is still so much of you that is Sharyl before canser. This goes without mentioning your personality. I'm not sure I know of anyone else who could go through this with such "sassiness." I'm not looking for compliments (so please don't bother with them). I'm just sharing what a friend said to me to show that sometimes we focus on a physical flaw that others don't even notice.

My last three chemo treatments went fine. I developed some strange nail infection as a result of one of the drugs I'm on, but antibiotics seem to be helping to clear it up. My nails are not so pretty though. I was told to put dark polish over them, but I kind of think that may have aggravated the problem, so I will leave them unpainted and just hide them as best as possible while out in public.

I thank God every day for each one of you. You motivate me to always keep my faith strong so that very soon I will step across the goal line and declare a victory in God's name and put canser as a bump in the road behind me. And when I look back on it, it will seem so small that I won't even notice it as a bump anymore.

Holding my head high and fighting like a cowgirl,
Sharyl

†

Sharyl, My Sister Survivor,
May the God of life be with you, calming your fears and teaching you to trust in his gracious love and mercy. May you be strengthened for your fight, and guided to choices for healing and wholeness. And may you be filled with joy and peace in experiencing God's presence on your journey. You are beautiful inside and out.

God bless,
Kelli

Thank You, Dinner Club

Wednesday, May 19, 2010

I have a group of girlfriends from high school, and we call ourselves "Dinner Club." Over the last 20 years or so, together we have created some pretty sweet memories.

We have celebrated marriages, births, graduations and promotions. We have comforted each other during the deaths of family members and lifted each other up when we needed it. Here is an example of how this group of girls supports one of their own.

As most of you know, I have been able to continue working while going through chemotherapy. Because I wear a wig daily, I tend to wear them out. I have thought about purchasing a human-hair wig a lot over the last year. The quality is better, so they last longer and look better.

Last week, my Dinner Club girlfriends organized a fundraiser so that I could buy a human-hair wig. I feel a little funny having a fundraiser held for what may be considered frivolous to some. But I know the intentions of my friends' hearts are to take away canser and chemo for me. Because they can't do that, this was a way they could help me obtain a good quality replacement for the hair that has fallen away.

They held a three-day garage sale—two days in the pouring rain—and raised more than enough money to get the wig I've been eyeing online for the last year. I've expressed my love and fondness for the community of South Saint Paul, and the garage sale held for me is another example of the wonderful people that live or have lived here. I will probably never know all of the people who donated items and supported the sale, but thank you all so very much.

I would like to extend a special thank you to my friends Bill and Kelly for opening up their garage and driveway for the sale. Hosting a garage sale is not an easy task, and I thank you for your kindness. Thank you to my friends who took time out of their busy schedules to organize and work at the sale. I'm hoping I won't have to wear a wig too much longer, but even if I were to stop chemo tomorrow, it would take another six months to achieve even the Halle Berry look again.

What I find a little amazing about this event is that I didn't find out about it until Friday afternoon when my husband drove me over to Bill and Kelly's house. Even as my friends greeted me in the driveway, I still didn't get what they had done or why, but I'm very grateful for their kindness and generosity. Anyway, thank you Dinner Club. I appreciate you girls more than you will ever know. I love you chicas—you make my heart smile!!!

I am reminded of some of the research about female friendships that I read in the book *The Girls from Ames* given to me by the Dinner Club last year. A Stanford University psychiatric study found that patients with advanced stages of breast canser were more likely to survive if they had a network of people with whom they could share their feelings.

I thank each of you who follow my CaringBridge site for your friendship and support. You all have demonstrated kindness to my family and me just by reading these updates, because you are allowing me to share my feelings with you. I cherish each friendship that I have in my life, whether you are a friend I have had since birth, like my brother or sisters, or someone I just met a few weeks ago at chemotherapy.

Life is sweet when you have friends to share it with.

Love,
Sharyl

†

>Sharyl,
>Perhaps we have found the author of our *Girls of Dinner Club* book, and she was there all along!
>I am so proud to have such a kick-butt friend!
>
>April

Rock Runners

Do you not know that in a race all the runners run,
but only one gets the prize?
Run in such a way to get the prize.
—1 Corinthians 9:24

Wednesday, May 26, 2010

I'm a huge reality TV fan. It's a guilty pleasure of mine. Sunday night was the finale of "Celebrity Apprentice." I had watched this show all season long and even before it was announced that Bret Michaels was hospitalized for a brain hemorrhage, he was starting to grow on me.

I've only seen clips of his show "Rock of Love," and as I watched "Celebrity Apprentice," it just didn't seem to me that they could be the same person. The Bret Michaels on "Celebrity Apprentice" was a hard-working, super creative, genuine, down-to-earth and gracious man, which I would like to believe is more representative of his personality.

I'm a card-carrying member of the 80's hair obsession society, and any self-respecting late 80's teenager who says they didn't rock out to a little Poison back in the day would be suffering from memory loss. Anyhow, I just can't seem to get Bret Michaels out of my head. Partly because of the fact that over the last few weeks he has been everywhere, but also because he reminds me that miracles do happen.

For some reason, I've been extremely emotional and confused over the past couple of weeks. It's almost as if I am suffering from PMS, pregnancy hormones, peri-menopause, or "sun-setting" as a friend's sister calls it. The only thing is that my sun set when they removed my ovaries, which means no hormones are running crazy through my body. So, I'm not sure what to make of my emotions.

A friend of mine who knew that I had been watching "Celebrity Apprentice" asked me the other day who I rooted for in the finale—Bret or Holly Robinson Peete. I told her I was a little torn. I like Holly's charity (an autism foundation), and I think she did an amazing job, but Bret really tugged on my heart strings. What he has overcome in the last few weeks is truly a miracle. I watched him gingerly walk onto the stage Sunday night and hug each contestant, and he seemed truly grateful to be there and to be alive. I was filled with emotion as he humbly accepted the compliments and well wishes from the other contestants and the audience.

My grandma, whom I never met, died of a brain aneurysm at the age of 36, so in my eyes he is truly a medical miracle, and my faith was restored that a miracle healing me of this canser crap is not far off. Based on fundraising merit alone, Holly should have won. But like I told my friend, Bret had to win. Everyone was emotionally rooting for him. He wasn't exactly the underdog, but in my opinion, Bret's win gave us all hope and restored in people (meaning me) the belief in miracles!

Last night, as I was doing some prayer journaling, I realized that I've been waiting to consider myself healed until a PET scan shows I'm healed. Jesus instructed us to live by faith and not by sight. I haven't been truly living by faith because like Thomas, I wouldn't believe in a healing until I have "proof" from a PET scan or a doctor tells me I'm healed. I'm sure you've all heard of the power of our minds in healing. There are many books, testimonies and scriptures about how powerful our minds are for our healing.

I have decided here and now that I do not need a report to tell me what I know to be true. I am strong and healthy, both physically and emotionally, and I thank God for giving me the strength to endure the treatments I've been receiving for the last year.

I ran a 5k last Saturday in 32 minutes, but I almost gave up with just 500 yards to go. Jason looked at me and said, "It's canser (a.k.a. the enemy) telling you that you can't finish. You are stronger and know better than that." Jason (a.k.a. my best friend) ran the whole way by my side, as he always does, cheering me on and never letting me give up.

I recently started doing a new exercise DVD. It's a great stretch and posture workout that incorporates bible scriptures. LOVE IT! I've done it a few times in the morning before work and it's an awesome way to start my day. But most days, I am not able to get up an extra hour early so I do it after work or in the evening. It's a great workout, and I highly recommend it. It's called "Power Praise Moves," and the website is praisemoves.com.

When I first watched the video, I thought, "This lady doesn't look like the usual fitness instructor," and I was a little concerned it wouldn't be challenging enough. (That's what I get for judging a book by its cover.)

At the end of the warm-up section, we do a move called rock runners. The accompanying scripture is Hebrews 12 1-2: *...And let us run with perseverance the race marked out for us, fixing our eyes on Jesus, the pioneer and perfecter of faith. For the joy set before him He endured the cross, scorning its shame, and sat down at the right hand of the throne of God.*

We finish the rock runners with this scripture from 1 Corinthians 9:24: *"Do you not know that in a race all the runners run, but only one gets the prize? Run in such a way that you get the prize."*

I have every intention of winning this race and using the victory to glorify God. Sometimes in a race, there may be stumbles or obstacles, but I will cross the finish line for a glorious win! And with the support, love and prayers of my family and friends, I don't see how I can lose.

I met with my doctor last week. She is a very smart, thorough, analytical and clinical doctor. We had a great conversation about the upcoming FDA approval of the PARP Inhibitors. These are the drugs that have proven to be very beneficial for people with the BRCA1 and BRCA2 genetic mutations. She said they will be available in June or July but that hopefully we won't have to use them.

The reason for going to the PARP Inhibitors would be progression, which is why she hopes we don't have to use them. I've found that my doctor doesn't tend to use the word "hope" a lot. I shared information about the webinar I watched from the Cancer Centers of America and what I got out of it. And as we were walking out of the room, I said to her, "And there's always hope," and she said to me, "Yes, there is always hope."

I bounced out of the building thinking, "Atta girl, doc!" and imagining the story she and I will have to share at her retirement party! (I think my doctor is about my age, maybe a little younger, so it will be a few years before she retires.)

Holding my head high and fighting like a cowgirl.

Yeehaw,
Sharyl

Cowgirls Dust Themselves Off

"Courage is being scared to death but saddling up anyway"
—John Wayne
(I've used this one before, but it's worth repeating)

Thursday, June 17, 2010

There is a song by Brooks and Dunn called "Cowgirls Don't Cry." Well, I believe cowgirls do cry sometimes, and it is perfectly okay. But, more importantly, I think cowgirls are very equipped to dust themselves off, get back on that horse and ride again.

I had a scan on Monday and met with my doctor yesterday. The results of the scan were not exactly what I was hoping for. It appears as though I have a few more spots on my liver that are looking to be canserous. In addition, I have a couple of the same lymph nodes faintly lighting up and a new lymph node that lights up near my pelvis.

The good news is that we are not out of treatment options. I've written in the past about the PARP Inhibitors, which have been very successful in reducing, stabilizing and removing canser from people who have triple-negative breast-canser metastases and the BRCA mutated genes. They have not been as successful with people who don't have both of those factors.

The drugs I was on were helpful in stabilizing and reducing/regressing canser in my body while the PARP Inhibitors were getting FDA approval. The PARP Inhibitors were fast-tracked through the FDA-approval process last year and have been given approval for what is called expanded access. In order to receive them for expanded-access use, you have to have triple-negative canser, the BRCA mutated gene and have tried a different form of chemotherapy.

The approval is expected on July 1st, so I'll be taking a couple of weeks off, which is good; I still need to recover from the stomach flu. The PARP Inhibitors have shown even better success when taken with two chemotherapy drugs. So, I will be taking the PARP Inhibitor, which is an oral drug, and have weekly infusions of carboplatin and gemzar—two Fridays in a row and then a Friday off.

The goal is to do this for anywhere from two to six months and then, when things are stabilized, we can remove the chemo drugs and stay on the PARPs for maintenance. Am I disappointed in this news? Of course. Am I discouraged? No. Have I lost my faith or hope? Absolutely not. This is just another bump in the road, but definitely not a road block. I still believe there will be a cure, and I know I will be healed.

A couple of weeks ago, I received a phone call from the South St. Paul American Cancer Society Relay for Life committee asking if I would like to be the 2010 Honorary Survivor for this year's Relay. I'm very honored to be selected by the committee, and I graciously accepted their request.

Over the last couple weeks I have been struggling emotionally, and I wasn't quite sure I was deserving of such an honor anymore. But what I have realized is that dealing with canser is a struggle. It is a struggle both physically and emotionally. As a daily fighter of canser, it is at times hard to hold my head high and not get discouraged, disappointed or upset. But while each day has its own challenges, it also has its own victories and immense joys.

Last week, I even helped to make a difference at our company. I brought to the attention of our executive vice president of human resources the struggle I was having with getting short-term-disability to pay for my three hours off each week for treatment. The head of the area that handles medical leaves contacted me, and we got the situation resolved. They are now working with our short-term disability provider to change our company's plan so that people with canser who are trying to continue to work during treatments will have no interruption in pay when it comes to balancing work and treatments. Yay!!!

Because I believe so strongly in a cure for canser and the efforts and support that the American Cancer Society provides people with canser and their caregivers, my family and friends and I will again have a team at this year's South St. Paul Relay for Life.

Holding my head high and fighting like a cowgirl.

God bless,
Sharyl

†

Hi Sharyl,

I can think of no one more deserving than you to represent our community at the Relay for Life. You have been an incredible inspiration to hundreds of people!

It's wonderful that you've shared all of your "up" moments with us, but even more importantly, you've shared some of the cloudier days too. It's what makes us human and by bouncing back from those times, you set the bar higher for all of us.

Anne

Trying My Best to Stay in Cowgirl Spirit

Wednesday, June 30, 2010

I had a little bit of a rough weekend. I have been battling stomach issues over the last four weeks. Late last week, I developed a fever. I called my oncologist's office on Friday, after I had used up every ounce of heat I could steal from Jason's body, and they told us to go to the ER.

It turns out my liver enzymes were elevated, which indicated a likely blockage in my biliary stent. I was admitted to the hospital, put on antibiotics, which brought my fever down, and then waited and waited until Sunday afternoon for the stent replacement.

This time it was a little more uncomfortable than normal. The doc saw something that concerned him, and he wanted me to stay the night for a CT scan in the morning. So, I got to see my little friend in CT, who I haven't seen in six months. We agreed we would much rather run into each other at Target, or somewhere like that, rather than in CT.

I got out of the hospital late Monday afternoon, and it was good to be home. My parents had brought a stuffed bear to me at the hospital Friday night. The guest services person wondered if they were visiting a grandchild, but, no, just their 39-year-old daughter. Yesterday, I noticed my dog trying to lay claim on my bear. He's taken over every other stuffed pet in our house, including the Webkinz and Joe Mauer bear. He spreads about a dozen animals throughout the house, but I told him this one was mine!

I wish I had some great news to share with you. But, for now, it is just status quo. I seem to have some fluid in my abdomen causing extreme bloating and pain, which makes it almost impossible to sleep. The CT scan showed multiple liver lesions like the PET scan indicated. They are small. I am waiting to get approval to start the study with PARP Inhibitors and carboplatin and gemzar. I am hoping for early next week.

I don't have anything insightful or deep to share with you today. I'm trying my best to stay in cowgirl spirit, but with some of the setbacks and pain, it's hard to find my smile. I know it's still in there and am hoping to find it this weekend at the cabin—near the water, my family, our harmless woodpeckers, our beautiful hummingbirds and, of course, the butterflies that never forget to visit while we are there.

I pray you all have a safe and happy Fourth of July holiday. If you have a vet in your life, don't forget to thank him or her for their service, as well. And pray for those who have not come home yet. God Bless America.

Trying to hold my head high and fight like a cowgirl,

Sharyl

†

Dear Sharyl,

Last night, I was working in the garden and was visited by several beautiful butterflies, many of them types I had not seen there before.

I stopped and witnessed their beauty and said a prayer for you with the hope that they would carry my words to your heart.

Nancy

PARP Inhibitors—Prayers, Please

Friday, July 16, 2010

I'm going to go out on a limb here and say that today I actually almost felt like a full-fledged cowgirl again. Yeehaw! It has been a long time since I could say that.

I've had a great day, all things considered. I got a good night's rest. (Yay.) I did not spend nearly every moment of my day in a chair in my basement. I got some work done around the house, some work done for Jason on the computer, went grocery shopping with Jason and the kids, and my biggest victory for the day: I went for a half-mile walk with the family and Blazer. My stomach was not in excruciating pain, and I think I even laughed and smiled a few times today.

I started chemo last week. I'm on a two-week on, one-week off schedule. On the first week, I get carboplatin and gemzar and on the second, I just get gemzar. I have tolerated the chemo well. Yesterday was my second day for this cycle. I have next week off.

The PARP Inhibitors have not been given approval for the expanded access protocol yet. My doctor called the doctor I spoke with at Mayo, and he is also waiting for their approval. We decided it was in my best interest to get started on chemo under the assumption that canserous lymph nodes in my abdomen are causing fluid to build up in my belly.

Because of the issues with my stomach, and the pain and the bloating, I haven't been able to eat well. As a result, I've lost some weight and since I'm carrying about three to five extra pounds of fluid in my belly, I've actually lost more than the scale indicates.

I can't feel good about losing weight without trying! My goal this week has been to carefully track what I eat so I can increase my calorie intake. I'm not good about taking pain meds, so my doctor prescribed a patch I wear daily to help alleviate the stomach pain. I decided there is no sense in being a martyr; I need to take care of myself, so if that means taking something stronger than an over-the-counter pain med, it doesn't make me weak, it makes me smart!

My doctor expects that by the end of the next chemo cycle my stomach will be better. As for the PARP Inhibitors, let's say some extra prayers that they get approval quickly. There is also a "lottery" involved with getting selected for the expanded-access protocol, so please say some prayers that I'm selected first to receive the drug.

I hope you all have a blessed weekend. I intend to make tomorrow even better than today has been. I thank you all for your support and the love you extend to my family and me during this bump in our road.

Holding my head high and fighting like a cowgirl,
Sharyl

†

Sharyl,

I often step near your garden stone from last year's Relay for Life, and I always say a prayer of thanks for your impact on so many others.

I pray that you and your family will be able to continue finding the smallest things to appreciate along this rollercoaster. Even when things aren't pretty, you seem to find the parts that are beautiful.

Robin

A Renewed Attitude and Cowgirl Spirit

Friday, August 6, 2010

I have been feeling pretty well; Leaps and bounds better than my last update. I've had two rounds of chemotherapy (four treatments). Last week, I had my stomach drained to remove two liters of fluid taking up residence in my belly. It was a huge relief to my stomach, and I lost about five pounds. Wow!

I still have some fluid, bloating, nausea and a little trouble digesting my food but I truly feel things are starting to get under control. I haven't been given the approval to start on the PARP Inhibitors yet, but our plan is to start in September after a couple more rounds of chemo. I will need to take three weeks off before starting the PARP drugs.

All in all, the most important thing is that I have more energy, better skin and eye color, my liver enzymes and bilirubin numbers are all either normal or getting very close, and I have a renewed attitude and spirit. I have a CT scan next Friday to compare to the one in late June. It's not the same as the PET, but it's a good measuring tool for now.

This is my final plug for this year's Relay for Life event. The Relay is tonight with the Opening Ceremony starting at 7 p.m. I will be sharing my story of hope, faith and belief for a life without canser. The event is open to the public, so come on down to share in this special evening, walk a lap in honor of a friend or family member, support the survivors as they take their laps, and/or share in the luminary ceremony to remember and honor all whose lives have been touched by canser.

Holding my head high and fighting like a cowgirl,
Sharyl

A Cowgirl with a Will to Survive

A Cowgirl with a Will to Survive

2010 Honorary Survivor Speech
South St. Paul—Relay for Life

Friday, August 6, 2010

My name is Sharyl Saver, and I am a three-year, two-time canser survivor. Some of you who may know me and read my CaringBridge website know that I also consider myself a cowgirl.

I'm deeply honored and grateful to stand before you today and share my story of hope, faith and belief for my future without canser. I would like to thank the Relay committee for choosing me as the 2010 South St. Paul Honorary Survivor.

I am a huge fan of this community. The support that comes from being a member of this town is far-reaching. And, what this Relay has done since its inception is nothing short of amazing. It says so much about our community and the top-notch people who live or have lived here.

I think back to the very first Relay, when at one point in the evening, the mayor announced how much money had been raised so far. I remember the chills that went through my body—and still get them today—when she said we had raised over $90,000 and that when the Relay committee started out on this venture, they had a goal of $30,000 based on our community size. I was filled with so much pride for this community that we more than tripled our goal!

My story with canser begins one spring morning in April of 2007. While getting ready for work, my son Jacob came into my room to give me a hug. He gently put his head on my chest, and I felt something tender. After enjoying the sweet hug from my youngest son, I touched the tender spot and felt a lump. Fear and panic set in.

I felt that lump over and over again for the next couple of days and made an appointment to have it checked out. My doctor decided that it warranted a mammogram, especially considering my family history. My maternal aunt, my mom and five of my maternal great grandmother's sisters all had breast canser. On Tuesday of the following week, I was told that I had breast canser.

I felt like I got punched in the gut. I was shocked, devastated and frightened. How could this be happening to me? My life was going great. I was 36-years old, happily married with three great children, a good job, awesome family and friends. I didn't have time for canser. My oldest son was about to graduate from high school. I had two small children and a life to live. But really, who has time for canser? So, we made decisions.

I went in for a bilateral mastectomy on May 7, 2007. When I woke up from surgery the first words out of my mouth were "Did it spread to my lymph nodes?" The nurse had to tell me "No" three times before I believed what she said. Even though I was in a lot of pain, I felt an amazing sense of joy. It was the kind of joy you experience when you hold your newborn baby in your arms for the very first time.

As I was transported to my recovery room, I was greeted by my family. I saw smiles on the faces of my husband, my father-in-law, my mom and my dad. I will never forget the joy in my dad's eyes. It's something I go back to often when I am feeling scared or defeated. Although the tumor was small, only 1 cm, and canser had not spread to my lymph nodes, it was a fast-growing type of canser, and it was recommended that I do four rounds of chemotherapy.

When I completed chemotherapy in September 2007, I thought I would be able to put this canser stuff behind me and carry on with my life. I began my breast reconstruction process in January of 2008 and completed the process in July of that year. My hair was starting to have a style again and my body was getting back to normal.

While I was receiving chemo in the summer of 2007, my doctor tested me to see if I was a BRCA carrier based on my family history with breast canser. The BRCA genetic mutations have been proven to increase a woman's lifetime risk of breast and ovarian canser. Not a huge shocker to me when the results came back that I am a carrier.

So, in addition to the breast canser blood screenings, my doctor had also been doing blood tests to screen for ovarian canser. And just as things were starting to get back on track, on October 20, 2008, I received a call from my doctor's office telling me my ovarian tumor marker test was elevated, and she wanted me to do a PET scan.

I spent the next six months going through many tests, and in May of 2009, I was diagnosed with a recurrence of breast canser that had metastasized to my liver and a couple of lymph nodes under my left arm. For the last year, I have been doing chemotherapy treatments to eradicate canser from my body.

I have always wanted to be able to call myself a cowgirl. Cowgirls are a tough breed. They may fall, but they always saddle up, hold their heads high and ride on. I thought you had to live on a ranch and own a horse to call yourself a cowgirl but I've learned being a cowgirl isn't about where you live, it's a state of mind.

I received a great book from a group of my friends last year entitled *Crazy Sexy Cancer Tips* by Kris Carr. This book is full of great insights from Kris and her "Cancer Posse," and at the end of the book Kris told me I was now a "Cancer Cowgirl." I would be okay with dropping the canser part and just calling myself a cowgirl.

Over this past year, I have made it my mission to help change the face of canser. To let people know that although canser may be a daily annoyance for some of us, we can still live productive and healthy lives. I have continued to exercise when I can, work (although I am taking a short break from work right now) and be a wife and mom—a hockey, football, dance, soccer and baseball mom, no less. All while receiving weekly chemotherapy treatments.

And, as some of you know, I love to jog and have had many "aha" moments while out running with my dog Blazer. I have had to put my jogging on hold for a couple of months but soon enough you will see me running around town again with my pink baseball hat and my pup.

This past year has been a struggle at times and on occasion my cowgirl spirit has been broken, but I have a great support network that helps restore my cowgirl and faith meters back to full. I have at times struggled with my reflection in the mirror, mainly because the reflection is a constant reminder that I am not out of the woods yet. I know I will get there, and for every day that I am here, they are one day closer to finding a cure.

My everyday life is filled with more joy than sadness, more hope than disappointment and more love than loneliness. I have awesome friends who encourage me and make me laugh. My parents, brother, sisters and in laws love me unconditionally, even when I have not deserved it—even when I have taken my fears and frustrations out on them. My children love me just because I am their mommy. And, I have my dear, sweet husband and best friend who always stands by my side, constantly cheers me on, never lets me give up, loves me every day, and still looks at me the same way as the day we married. He is my rock and my strength. So, all in all, I would say I am abundantly blessed.

Over the last year, my faith has strengthened deeply. I am not sure how you could get through a bump in the road like this without faith and hope. As a result, I have been so much more aware of the rainbows in my life. Rainbows to me are like a promise of faith and hope that although we may experience rain in our lives, some of the most spectacular beauty is created as a result of the rain. And in the words of my favorite little cowgirl, Dolly Parton, "If you want the rainbow, you gotta put up with the rain!"

I would like to thank you all for participating in the Relay. On behalf of the survivors in a daily battle to overcome canser, your support, belief and hope in the Relay that one day soon there will be a cure for canser is greatly appreciated. For the survivors who every day are putting canser that much farther in the past so that their bump in the road is barely recognizable anymore, Relay is helping to ensure that canser will never be in their futures.

For the caregivers who tirelessly devote themselves to their loved ones, Relay is about realizing a dream come true. And for those who have passed on, Relay is about a promise that we will never forget them or what a difference they made in our lives. I believe that we are making a difference and that the efforts of the Relay for Life will eventually lead to a life where canser is but a distant memory.

At the end of the book *Crazy Sexy Cancer Tips,* Kris Carr says (paraphrased a bit) that "being a canser cowgirl or cowboy is being a part of a divine order, a free-spirited bunch of powerful people who take charge as we gallop through life's obstacle course. We don't whisper, we ROAR! We are heavenly creatures full of sass and fireworks. We are dazzling warriors full of peace and fury."

I strive every day to live up to this description. Some days I fall short and others I live up to it beyond my expectations. But mostly, I'm proudly just a cowgirl with a will to survive.

This year's Relay is about celebrating more birthdays. I look forward to celebrating my 40th birthday on Tuesday and many more birthdays in the years to come.

Have a super night and God bless!

Sharyl Saver

✝

Sharyl,

You were amazing tonight at the Relay for Life! You should be so proud of who you are, what you stand for and how great of a cowgirl you are! I feel privileged to know you!

You looked beautiful standing up there with your gorgeous hair and fashionable glasses. I almost forgot where we were for a minute and thought the paparazzi would be jumping out to take your picture!

Happy Birthday a few days early! Congratulations, and thank you for allowing me to shed tears of joy for you tonight! Yeehaw!

Love,
Jen

Laughing and Smiling Again

Wednesday, August 18, 2010

Yippee! I got my CT scan results this morning. All the liver lesions are decreasing in size or remaining stable. The ones that are stable are most likely not canserous anyway. The CT scan doesn't distinguish between canserous and non-canserous lesions.

The scan also showed that the fluid in my belly is almost all gone, so I was able to start my third cycle of chemotherapy this morning. And, the treatment is going in the right direction. My doctor told me the PARP Inhibitors expanded-access protocol is now open, and I will be starting sometime in October. I just need to get a couple more cycles of chemo in my body before taking a three-week break to start the PARPs.

After the Relay, I lost a considerable amount of weight. But, since I hadn't been eating well at all for the last eight weeks, and the fluid had finally flushed out of my system, I think I finally had a true representation of the actual weight I have lost. I am slowly putting the pounds back on and hope by Labor Day to be back to a "good weight." (I could do without the "I have some pounds I could give you" jokes. If it were only that simple...)

I've been regaining my physical strength each day. I have been able to get out of the chair and do more with my kids, and I have been getting out for short walks. All of this, along with the great news of my scan, and my spirit and attitude are renewed. It feels awesome to laugh and smile and surround myself with things that have nothing to do with canser!

We are off to our happy place, where "life is good" and where the water is warm, the loons are singing, the fish are biting and nature is healing!

Holding my head high and fighting like a cowgirl!
Sharyl

p.s. This is a photo of my sister Jean and me when she made a surprise visit from Alaska back to Minnesota, and we went to the cabin for the weekend.

†

Sharyl,
That is awesome news! Yeehaw! Keep your spirits up and remember I am always there for you. You are very strong and your light always shines. I love you.

Your big sister from Alaska,
Jean

†

Hi Sharyl,
We always ask for God's answer yesterday, but if we that would happen, we would never seek Him in thoughtful prayer. We would only seek Him as we would order a Big Mac from the drive through. Patience and trusting in His plan for us is our cross to bear. He is with you, always.

Deb

Happy 40th Birthday to Me!

Tuesday, August 24, 2010

My husband threw me a great surprise birthday party Saturday night. Although I basically went kicking and screaming because he brought me home early from my happy place, it was one of the most fun nights I've had in a super long time. I needed it. I needed to be out socializing with family and friends. I felt great, and I looked good, if I do say so myself!

As I embark on this next half of my life, many thoughts come to mind. The first being that throughout this last year I've been slightly obsessed with wanting to "go back." I've had this feeling before. For instance, I wish so many times that I could go back to February 24, 2000 and start over. That was the day our daughter, Caylin, was born.

I would have done so many things differently. I would have taken video. I would have done a CaringBridge website. I would have researched more. I would have fought harder for her. And, I would have taken more pictures. It breaks my heart that I don't have one picture of my dad and my sweet Caylin together.

Over the last year, I have longed for the woman I was before I had canser. I've desired to be the long-haired, somewhat care-free mom and wife I was when I was 36. Or, I have wished to be the woman who was piecing her life back together after an initial canser diagnosis and just starting to regain her confidence at the age of 38.

But life is not about going back and is so much more about living in the moment and moving forward. We should cherish the memories we've made along the way and learn from the mistakes we've made, but not spend too much time beating ourselves up for them. And, we cannot get caught up in the "what ifs" and the "shoulda, coulda, wouldas."

There is a new show on Showtime called "The Big C." (I don't get Showtime, so I can't watch it.) The gist of the show is that the main character is diagnosed with canser and only has a couple of years so she makes big changes in her life to really start living. I don't need to make the kind of changes she chooses to make, but I have decided with the help of my friend that we are going to work on publishing and sharing my story in a book. It will be inspired by my CaringBridge posts.

I saw the actress, Laura Linney, from the show "The Big C," being interviewed on one of the morning news shows, and I'm not sure if it was her character, another character or Laura herself that said, "Aging is not a right, it's a priviledge." Although it's kind of a sad statement, it's true. The reality of this world is that some people die young, and we should view getting older as a blessing—from the wisdom we have gained to the accompanying wrinkles, battle scars, stretch marks, sags and gray hairs. Fortunately, I don't have gray hair or too many laugh lines. And in one particular area of my body, I will never sag! But I don't seem to care about any of that.

Maybe it's because my doctor diagnosed me as terminal. (For the record, we are all terminal.) Maybe it's because I have dealt with the physical side effects of chemo and how they transform your appearance. I appreciate the beauty and strength that God gave me inside. And I embrace the beauty of my soul and how I can use it to inspire and lift up others, versus worrying about whether I could still be compared to beauties such as Jenny McCarthy or Kim Bassinger.

So far, I love being 40. I was actually very much looking forward to turning 40. I think your 40's bring something that other decades didn't. There is a self confidence in me that I didn't have when I was 30. I have much more wisdom than I did 10 years ago. And besides, 40 is the new 30 anyway...

I'm so excited to see what the next 40 years brings to my family and me. Thank you to the family and friends who shared in my birthday party. You made the night so special and fun. I love you,

Jason, with all my heart. Sorry I was mad at you—I loved my surprise party. You make my heart smile.

Thanks to the Lid Twisters for keeping us entertained. I know my "Cowboy Boots" dance wasn't up to its usual energetic level, but I won't stop believing that I'll be back to full throttle before long. Maybe my new pink and brown cowgirl boots will help me next time I hear the song. (Thanks, Di Di, they make me smile just looking at them, and I feel ever so strong in them!!!)

Have a great week! Holding my head high and fighting like a cowgirl!!!

God bless,
Shar

✝

Hey Cowgirl,
Happy, happy birthday to you, my strong, beautiful and inspirational sister!

Love now and always,
Dianna

It's Good to Be Back at Work

Wednesday, September 15, 2010

Last week when I went in for chemo, I met with the nurse practitioner. She had a note from my doctor explaining that she wanted me to get everything in order so I could get in the lottery drawing for the expanded-access study to receive the PARP Inhibitor. So, they drew labs on Thursday before chemo like they always do, and I had to have an EKG done before Tuesday (yesterday) so I could be put in the study pool.

Unfortunately, I did not get put in the pool this week because my hemoglobin is not high enough. It needs to be at least 9, and I have been hovering around 8.3 to 8.7. I was at 8.7 last Wednesday. They wanted me to get retested on Monday. I had very serious doubts that the number would go up since I just received chemo and usually I like being right, but in this situation I would much rather have been wrong. My hemoglobin was at 8.4. So, we will try again tomorrow when they draw my labs and hope that the additional iron sources I have been eating will have helped to boost my hemoglobin so that I can get in the pool next Tuesday.

The way the study works is that you're put in a pool, and then they do lottery drawings each Tuesday to select participants. The study is open to women with a BRCA mutation who have triple-negative breast canser that has metastasized and who have tried other chemotherapy treatments, which haven't worked. They will be taking as few as 750 and as many as 1,500 patients, and the study is open to anyone in the country with the above criteria.

There is no guarantee I will get in the study unless, in the meantime, it is given FDA approval and can be prescribed just like any other chemotherapy drug. This is the main goal of the study and the trial. I don't know where they are in the approval process, but it's my understanding they are still trying to fast track it, which could still mean anywhere from six months to five years.

I am halfway through my first week back at work. I feel good, and it feels so awesome to be back at work. The decision for me to take a leave of absence was very difficult, especially emotionally. It took me five weeks to make the decision and what prevented me from taking the leave was that work was one thing that was just me.

In my mind, if I took a leave, I was allowing canser to beat me. My body needed rest, there was no question about that, but by taking a rest from work, my mind and spirit took a beating as well. In the back of my mind, I was afraid that if I took a break, I was never going back and that this was just the beginning of the end. And then while on leave, I wasn't feeling better. In fact it seemed like things were getting worse. I wasn't eating, and I was throwing up A LOT. I spent about 10 weeks getting just 800 calories a day in my body and that was before I threw up.

But I truly believe I experienced a miracle in August. All of sudden on August 20th, I just stopped throwing up. And as one day turned into two days and then into a week and then into three weeks, and as I got my appetite back and my strength started to return, I started to feel better and better until by Labor Day I was back to a good weight. I went from consuming about 800 calories a day to consuming about 3,000. I swear I am hungry from the minute I get up to the minute I fall asleep.

Sweet story. Last Friday night, it was about 10:30 and my tummy was grumbling. Taylor came into my bedroom after his shift at Angelo's Pizza, and all I could smell was pizza. I thought to myself, "Please say you brought home a pizza," but when he said he was going to go out with some friends, I knew he hadn't brought one home. I told him the next day about what I'd been thinking and he asked if he should bring one home tonight after work. Being a martyr, I said, "No. I shouldn't really be eating that late anyway."

But in true Taylor fashion and being the wonderful son that he is, at 10:30, when my stomach was grumbling again, he walked in with a sausage, tomato, onion, black olive and hot-pepper ring pizza. I was in heaven! Oh how I missed tomatoes this past summer.

Tomatoes and anything made with them are a staple in my diet, and I tried and tried to eat them over the summer and each time I did, I paid a major price but thank God they are my friends again!

Anyway, I decided it was time for me to get back to work so that I could begin feeling even more like normal. I am starting out working four hours a day and then in a few weeks will return to my normal schedule of six hours a day. I was welcomed back by my boss and coworkers this week. It is great to see them, and they all had such kind things to say about my return.

They have been so awesome about covering for me while I was out. I told one of my coworkers how I was hungry all the time, and he said, "Well that's good because we seem to have cake every other day here lately" and in true welcome-back fashion, we celebrated my return with a cake!

Even though I didn't win the PARP lottery this week, I feel like I have won the lottery in getting my life, my appetite, my weight and, most of all, my fighting cowgirl spirit back!

God bless. Holding my head high and fighting like a cowgirl,
Sharyl

Wearing My Boots Today

Thursday, September 16, 2010

I wore my new cowgirl boots to work and chemo today and got lots of smiles and compliments on them. I think wearing my boots fit my attitude, and that all the prayers being said on my behalf, and the threat from my nurse to the lab lady that she better bring back a hemoglobin number of 9 or higher worked!

My sweet, little nurse came back after about 15 minutes and gave me two thumbs up. 9 right on the nose! Hip hip hooray for pumpkin seeds and Special K! Everyone in the office was excited. My doctor, the nurses and the clinical research nurse were so excited to see my number. The lottery is actually done on Wednesdays. So far no one in the MOHPA network has been selected, but with my army of earth angels and my kick-butt attitude, we will just see what happens.

God bless and thank you! Holding my head high and fighting like a cowgirl!

Sharyl

Sounds Like a Challenge to Me

Thursday, October 7, 2010

My mom was looking through her many pictures from over the years and came across this photo of me as a little girl.

As a young girl, I was fascinated with my dad's boots. In my opinion, my dad was the strongest man I knew. (Now he and Jason are tied for "strongest man" in my life.) I loved my dad's boots, and my sister and I would share the honor of helping him take them off when he got home from work.

Here is the observation from my mom when she sent me the picture: "I'm sending you this picture of you trying to walk in Dad's boots. It reminds me of how you were determined to walk in those boots and didn't give up; just like you have always been determined to succeed in spite of circumstances. Keep that determined attitude and keep walking in those boots. —Love, Mom"

For those of you who know me, you know that like everyone else I have had my share of challenges, starting with becoming a single mom at the age of 18 and then attending college and graduating from the University of Thomas with a degree in accounting just three short years later. However, those two things could not have been accomplished without the love and support of my parents, siblings, grandma and aunt.

I remember a teacher in high school who learned of a young senior girl becoming a mother and said her future was ruined and that she'd never be able to attend college. I heard her words in my head all the while I was attending the university as a single mom.

Tell me I can't do something, and I don't take it as truth, but as a challenge. I just pulled myself up by my boot straps.

Then, in my late 20's, at what was supposed to be a turning point in my life, I married the man of my dreams. After dating a number of not-good-enough-to-be-Taylor's-step-dad type of guys, along came Jason. When Jason asked me to marry him, I said, "Yes," and then immediately followed it with, "Can we have a baby right away?" His response was "Of course."

We were blessed just eight and half months later with one of the most beautiful baby girls ever. The blister on her finger and leg were of no concern to me; she was perfect. Two days after she was born, we learned she had a disease for which there is no cure and that technically our faulty DNA had caused it. My soul mate and I were told there was a one in a million chance of us both having this genetic mutation. More annoying data!

Before Jason and I celebrated our first anniversary, we buried our first-born child. Talk about devastation. Nothing and no one will ever fill the place in our family that she held; our family will always feel incomplete as a result of her leaving this earth prematurely. But once again, we had to put on our boots and keep on going. We had Taylor to take care of and we had each other—and we believed we would go on to have healthy children.

I was watching a show the other night that gave the statistic that 80% of marriages with a special-needs child end in divorce. I've also heard that same statistic for couples who lose a child and for couples where one spouse has canser. So, do Jason and I have a 240% chance of ending up divorced? I say "HECK NO." Those are just numbers, and numbers can be manipulated to say anything.

If any of you are facing these situations, I say BALONEY. You and your spouse were brought together for a reason and maybe it's to be the support each other needs. And to quote Matthew 18:20, *"For where two or three gather in my name, there am I with them."*

Stay strong and stay united.

When I was diagnosed with a recurrence of breast canser, my doctor told me she couldn't offer me a cure. She could only offer me treatments and at some point the treatments will no longer work and canser will take my life. Sounds like a challenge to me. Canser is evil, canser is mean and canser is UGLY. But I believe canser can be overcome. I believe I will survive. I believe that with faith in God and the medical advancements in the field of canser, I will beat this nasty disease.

I overheard one of the nurses talking to a patient last week, and she said she would love to be out of job as a result of researchers discovering a cure for canser. I sure hope we can push her out of the canser-maintenance field and put her into the canser-curing field. So, I put on my boots and promised to overcome this silly canser and succeed in spite of this circumstance.

Each time I am faced with a difficult circumstance, I am reminded of and able to draw upon my faith to get through the challenge. I also am reminded that I am surrounded by so many prayers and loving and supportive family members and friends. I thank God for each one of you every day!

Today, I'm wearing my pink cowgirl boots because I got a call from the research nurse at my clinic yesterday, and I was selected to participate in the PARP Inhibitor study! From the literature I've read, I can be on the study for 12 months. (In the meantime, hopefully the drug will be approved.) I'll add two more chemo dates to my existing treatment plan where I just get the PARP Inhibitor. So, in the span of two weeks, I will have chemo four times. I believe this will be the cure for me and for the small minority of women who share the same type of canser and mucked-up gene as me.

As many of you know, October is Breast Canser Awareness month, and I say wear your pink proudly (or yellow or whatever color is associated with the canser you want awareness for) so that together we can eradicate this enemy and put my nurse into another line of work.

Holding my head high and fighting like a cowgirl,
Sharyl

†

Congratulations! I am so happy for and proud of you. I've been wearing my pink ribbon every day this month and have plenty of pink support clothing I'm wearing proudly as well. I think of you daily and send you strength through the bracelet. I believe in you! Good luck with the trial.

Love,
Jeannie

†

Sharyl,
You just keep wearing those pink boots; I think they bring you good luck. I am so happy for you!

Love You,
Nancy

My Cup Overflows

Disappointing News

Sunday, October 10, 2010

Well, I was given disappointing news on Friday. I've been experiencing some headaches, which I assumed were just sinus headaches. When I mentioned them to my doctor, she wanted me to have an MRI just to be safe. On Friday, I was supposed to see the nurse practitioner at my oncologist's office for an exam to get started with the study.

I got a call about an hour and half before my appointment from my doctor's nurse, and she said that I would instead be seeing my doctor and that I needed to bring someone along with me to the appointment.

I spent the next hour and half freaking out. Jason was at the cabin and wouldn't be able to make it back in time, so my mom came with me as he headed home. My doctor shared that I have canser cells in my cerebral spinal fluid. The canser cells that try to invade my body are aggressive and look for any place they can hide. And for some reason, the chemo drugs I am getting now cannot cross the blood-brain barrier to reach the fluid around the brain and spine.

I have to see a surgeon this week to have a catheter placed in my head so that the chemo drugs that target this type of canser can be administered directly to the cerebral spinal fluid. I will be getting a different drug than what I am on now to treat the canser cells in the fluid.

Unfortunately, this also means I will not be able to participate in the study but my doctor believes the PARP Inhibitors will have FDA approval by January or February. So, the PARP Inhibitors will be delayed for me.

I am obviously deeply devastated and, I'm not going to lie, I'm scared too. But, I still believe that I will continue to survive for a very long time and be cured of canser. I am ever so grateful for all of your love, support and prayers.

Holding my head high and fighting like a cowgirl.

God bless,
Sharyl

†

Sharyl,

I can't begin to imagine the disappointment you feel. You inspire me and so many others with your courage, yet I would rather be uninspired than for you to have to live one more day with canser.

You are an amazingly strong woman and like all of the other canser cowgirls out there, you deserve a canser-free life! I am praying for you to overcome this setback and see the benefits of the PARP Inhibitors.

Leah

✝

The LORD is my shepherd, I lack nothing. He makes me lie down in green pastures, He leads me beside quiet waters, He refreshes my soul. He guides me along the right paths for His name's sake. Even though I walk through the darkest valley, I will fear no evil, for you are with me; your rod and your staff, they comfort me.

You prepare a table before me in the presence of my enemies. You anoint my head with oil; my cup overflows. Surely your goodness and love will follow me all the days of my life, and I will dwell in the house of the LORD forever.
—Psalm 23

When Pastor was reciting this to us today, I thought of you. It's a reminder that our Heavenly Father is always with us through life's trials. Our reward is to share eternity with Him.

Love,
Nana Sue and Papa Steve

My Cup Overflows
—Psalm 23:5

Monday, October 25, 2010

Last Monday, I had an Ommaya Reservoir put in my head. It involved the drilling of eight holes into my skull so that a surgical halo could be attached with screws. The halo was to keep my head still during placement of this special kind of port, which will allow for chemo drugs to be infused directly into my cerebral spinal fluid. I then had an MRI and CT scan to take pictures of my head to guide port placement.

Then it was off to surgery. They had to shave my head before doing the surgery. :-(I will be going as Frankenstein for Halloween this year. With the 14 stitches on top of my head, the four stitches on my forehead and four in the back of my head, I look a little scary. You know it's bad when the best compliment someone can come up with is, "You have a really nice-shaped head." That would be great if I were a man trying to pull off the bald look.

As of right now, my treatment regimen goes like this: I will receive methotrexate for the canser in my cerebal fluid twice a week. Then, hopefully in about three weeks when it looks as though the fluid does not show anymore canser, I will switch drugs and only have chemo once a week. And I will still get the drug carboplatin once a week for two weeks and then get a week off from that drug.

It has been an emotional struggle over the last few weeks dealing with the spread of canser in my body, but I've been reminded of the love that I'm surrounded by every day from my family and friends. The love and support from you all is beyond amazing. I am grateful for each and every one of you.

I thank you for what you do for my family and me. For your prayers, meals, inviting my kids to spend time with you, house cleaning, emails, phone calls, texts and cards. From Psalm 23:6, *"Surely your goodness and love will follow me all the days of my life..."*

Holding my head high and fighting like a cowgirl.

God bless,
Sharyl

†

Sharyl,

I know things might not look so good right now, and this bump in the road is certainly not what you wanted to deal with, but please remember that so many people love and care about you and also believe in your strength and determination.

We are all here beside you or behind you, whatever you need. You hang in there and lean on those who love you and care so much! I believe someday you will look at this time as just another bump in the road that you "cruised over."

Take care,
Mary

Promising PET Results

Saturday, November 6, 2010

"Conclusion: Partial metabolic response with the hepatic metastases showing significant decrease in size and metabolism and the metastatic left axillary, porta hepata, mesenteric and retroperitoneal lymph nodes no longer visualized."

These are the results from the PET scan I had this Wednesday compared to the PET I had in June when I was told I had a progression of canser. That PET showed that I had multiple liver (hepatic) lesions (between 6 to 10) and lymph nodes that light up under my left arm (axillary), porta hepata (liver), mesenteric and retroperitoneal (abdomen). I also had an infection at that time, which put me in the hospital for a weekend in late June. (Infections can light up lymph nodes.)

This PET scan is great news in my opinion. PET scans do not show brain-fluid activity, but my nurse practitioner takes fluid out before my treatment to see if it still contains canser cells. My treatment plan is: brain-fluid chemo injections every other week, with the goal of going down to once a month. Continue with the liver treatments of two weeks on and one off of two chemo drugs.

We are hoping and praying for the PARP Inhibitors approval as soon as possible. My doctor found out the PARPs do cross the blood-brain barrier, so I will not need to continue with the brain injections once I can receive them.

Holding my head high and fighting like a cowgirl. Take care and God bless.

Love,
Sharyl

Rest in Peace, Elizabeth Edwards

Saturday, December 11, 2010

My heart and prayers go out to Elizabeth Edwards' family and friends as they deal with her passing. Her death seems to have hit me a little harder than I would've expected. Canser is so annoying.

It was also hard to hear of my young friend, who is having to start treatment for canser again this week. It saddens me that she is dealing with canser when she should be stressing out over tests or what she is going to wear to a party this weekend. I know that she will be healed of canser and has a wonderful and bright future ahead of her. (Who knows; maybe even as my future daughter-in-law. I'm just saying…I am totally kidding you two.)

Also, I heard of another strong, inspirational woman who has had to deal with canser for a while who received frustrating and disappointing news this week. My prayers go out to these women and their families. May God bless you both with hope, faith and unconditional love.

Canser frustrates and baffles me. With all the brilliant researchers and scientists and the endless amounts of money donated for research, why can't they figure this out? I know I have a simple brain and canser is much more complicated than my mind can comprehend. And, I know they have come a long way in treatments and can even "cure" some cansers. For every day I am here, they are closer to new treatments and a cure, but I sure wish it wasn't about making a profit. Instead, I wish all researchers would work together for the good of those of us whose lives are at stake. But I digress…

Ms. Edwards' passing hit me hard because I too was diagnosed with Stage 4 metastatic breast canser. We have different types of breast canser but they both spread to other areas of the body, which stinks and is no good. When I heard on the news Monday that she was gravely ill, I thought, "Oh crap."

I had just said to my mom the week before, "Elizabeth Edwards is obviously still doing well because we haven't heard anything about her in awhile." I look to other Stage 4 metastatic survivors on my down days as a reminder that we can survive for a long time with this "chronic disease."

So, Ms. Edwards' news was shocking to me. I was having trouble sleeping that night and wanted to watch TV, and I went downstairs to lie on the couch. I woke up the next morning to Robin Roberts, a breast canser survior herself, and a doctor talking about Ms. Edwards. The doctor said that when canser comes back to other areas of the body, it is no longer curable, only treatable, and with each new treatment, the ability of the drugs to kill or outsmart the canser goes down, but the side effects go up.

Well, "Good Morning" to you too. Guess that's what I get for having the TV on while sleeping. None of this information was news to me—I just don't need to be reminded of it.

I once peeked on the Livestrong website and took the "What are your chances?" quiz. It said I only have a 25% chance of surviving more than five years. My young friend with a survival statistic higher than 25% said she believes she will be in the percentage that survives. I too believe I will be in the percentage that survives. Like I told my mom a week ago, someone has to be in the surviving percentage, so why not me? I seem to excel when percentages are against me.

I'm feeling pretty well. And, I feel much better emotionally as the week has progressed. I have been either out with or have been contacted by people who are so good for my soul, and who have boosted my mood. I don't have tons of energy. I decided not to go back to work yet. This surgery on my head has taken longer to recover from than I would've expected. It doesn't help that I haven't had a break from chemo since I had the procedure.

I had my first chemo injection in my head the day after the surgery. I still receive my regular chemo, two weeks on and one week off, and I continued with that treatment the day after I got out of the hospital. So, I decided I need to save my energy for taking care of myself and keeping up with my kids.

My hair is growing back fast, dark and thick. I have over an inch now. But every time I go for an injection, they shave the injection site, which is right on top of the front of my head. It looks like a cartoon character bump! I found a couple of gray hairs, which Jason said he couldn't see at first and then a little while later said, "You do have some gray hairs." I reminded him that his hair is so dark, you can barely tell he once was a red head, so take that!

Oh, and as for the cerebral spinal fluid, I still have canser cells in there, but it's just a "yes" or "no" test. It doesn't measure whether the canser is decreasing. I will continue with every-other-week injections until the answer is no. Then we will go down to once-a-month injections. I pray that the fluid she took out yesterday gives a clear no. That would be a perfect Christmas present.

I hope you all are enjoying and find much love, joy, blessings and miracles during this beautiful holiday season. In the words (paraphrased a bit) of Bill Murray in my favorite Christmas movie, *Scrooged*:

> "The miracle of Christmas is not just once a year…it's the one time of year we all act a little nicer, we smile a little easier and we give cheer a little more…everybody has to have this miracle happen to them…It's a really great feeling…and if you like it and you want it, you'll get greedy for it, and you will want it every day of your life."

I am thankful for the blessing and gift that each one of you is to my family and me. God bless you. Holding my head high and fighting like a cowgirl.

Sharyl

Merry Christmas from the Saver Family

†

Sharyl,

I miss your bright smile at the office but am so happy you're home taking care of yourself and your family! Your family Christmas picture made me smile huge when I saw it! You have an absolutely beautiful family! As a fellow hockey lover, I must say your wardrobe choice was perfect!

You're in my thoughts and prayers constantly. Not just at Christmas, but always. You have an energy and light to you that is so bright and beautiful it touches people far beyond your reach. Keep shining and have a very Merry Christmas!

Blessings and love to you and your family!
Kari

Moment in Time

Saturday, January 8, 2011

Last week I went to the clinic to get my head injection, and I had a horrible headache that day. I mentioned it to the nurse so she told my nurse practitioner, who didn't want to do the injection because she could see the pain in my eyes. Instead, she sent me over to have a CT scan of my head and also to have an ultrasound on my arms, since I have had some swelling in my left arm. She was looking for possible blood clots in my arm or head and swelling in my head.

The tests showed that everything is okay. My arm did not show any blood clots; I most likely have lymphedema in it. Then, she wanted me to have an MRI to check the status of the cerebral spinal fluid the next day. The MRI showed that all of the original spots were getting smaller, but there may be a new spot. Personally, I'm not terribly concerned about this "new spot."

My gut has told me before when to be concerned: when I was initially diagnosed, when I had a recurrence and when I had my first MRI. However, my nurse practitioner would like to take a more aggressive approach, and we are changing my drugs and the frequency with which I receive them.

So I have a new unpaid job at my oncology clinic; I will be spending three days a week there as a pin cushion and drug receiver. And then I still have my night and weekend job as a hockey mom and chauffeur. Although it has been sad that because of some side effects of the chemo medications I put in my body every week, I've had to call in sick at my hockey-mom job. I don't care about missing a practice, but to miss a game breaks my heart.

I still seem to tolerate chemo fairly well, but since I have canser cells in my cerebral spinal fluid, I still tend to get headaches. I have occasional dizzy spells, which are usually brought on earlier in the day if I have too much coffee and not enough food. I've always had food issues like that, but before it just made me crabby, and now it makes me dizzy. And, unfortunately, I don't have the exercise energy I once had.

On the flip side, my doctor is always amazed that despite not receiving a white-cell booster shot, my white blood cells are always well into the normal range. I firmly believe that partly has to do with my eating habits, which are not nearly as good as they used to be, and even though I haven't been able to exercise very much for the last six months, the 20 years of exercising I had done prior to this has been beneficial in my treatment.

When I was 17, my boyfriend at the time bought me a gym membership. Now some may have been offended by such a gift, but I fell in love with it, even though it was a membership to what most would call a "muscle-head" gym. Only myself and about 10 other women had memberships, yet surprisingly I was not intimated by all those body builders, and I loved the atmosphere. So much so that after quitting while attending college, it was one of the first things I bought once I got my first post-college job.

Not being able to exercise regularly makes me sad. My favorite exercise DVDs are way too intense for me—even those I would consider very low-impact make me out of breath. My favorite DVD lady can't even make stretching videos that aren't hard. Ugh. So my goal for this year is to start exercising regularly again.

I'm going to begin with some good old-fashioned mall walking (because walking outside in Minnesota really stinks in the winter) and build back up so that hopefully in six months or so my favorite DVD lady and I can be "friends" again. I say friend loosely because even when I was in great shape, I often yelled at her.

On a very sad note, my condolences go out to the friends and family of Melissa, who lost her battle against breast cancer this week. The world has lost one special earth angel and heaven has gained a wonderful soul.

I watched a show on the History Channel the night before Easter, and it talked about the gospel of Thomas. I haven't read it, but it basically said Thomas spoke of the parallels and closeness of our earthly world and the heavenly world and how we are much closer and connected than we think.

This brought much comfort to me and made sense. When it is said that your loved one will always be with you, I believe this is so true. I also believe that if it helps you get through the day of grieving to say that your loved one is with you and shares in your triumphs and pains, there is nothing wrong with that. Besides, there are too many personal and unexplainable gifts that come our way, suggesting that our loved ones are with us and their love, if we are open to it, can provide us with some comfort until we meet again.

On the next page is a poem I wrote after my daughter Caylin passed away. I tailored it to Melissa.

God bless. Holding my head high and fighting like a cowgirl.

Love,
Sharyl

Moment in Time

Every day, I think of that moment in time,
when I could feel your hand in mine.
I am reminded of the way you looked into my eyes,
searching for an answer why.

You were graceful to the end,
and should not have had to be so brave.
But faith, hope and love is the beauty
your life has taught me to believe.

Still, I go back to that moment in time,
when you were here
and we thought everything would be fine.
You came into our lives as an answered prayer,
but "there is no cure,"
are words no one will ever be prepared to hear.

I am sorry this wasn't the way we had planned it to be,
we should be at home together as a family.
At night I dream you wrap your hand around mine,
and lead me to that moment in time.

You tell me you are still here with me,
not only in my memories and in my heart.
But also in the beauty of lilies
and whispers of butterfly wings.
We will never be far apart.

From there you lead me to that moment in time,
where you are now,
where you laugh and play with Jesus,
the angels and the children around.

*You show me how you play on heaven's fairway,
then we sit by the lake and you tell me about your day.*

*I know you are safe, happy and surrounded by love,
I believe you are watching over me from heaven above.*

*Now we have come to that moment in time,
when I must stay behind.
I feel you leaving the embrace of my arms.
As you look up, I see your sweet smile.*

*You gently wipe away the tear from my face,
please don't cry,
I promise we will be together again one day
are the words you say, to comfort my fears
and remind me you will visit me again in my dreams.*

*In the morning when I wake,
I reminisce of the journey we made.*

*I know there will be joy in my day,
and I am thankful for the Gift of God's Grace,
which gives me strength and reminds me
that even still, in this moment of time,
your love in my heart will always be felt.*

—*Sharyl Saver*

An Alternate Route to the Cure

Thursday, January 20, 2011

It's time to make a change in my treatment plan. I had a PET scan on Tuesday of this week, and my liver metastases have gotten a little darker and larger and the ones under my arm showed up again. The good news is that nothing new showed up on the scan. So, I will be switching to an oral chemo drug, which I will take two times a day for two weeks and then take a week off.

I had to choose between two different drugs, and I decided to take the drug with less side effects. My hope is that by taking this drug, I may regain more energy and become more active, which will in turn help my mood and spirit.

I'm hoping for good news from my appointment today that the cerebral spinal fluid shows no more canser cells so that I will be able to take a break from the head injections. Thank you for all your prayers and support. Our family appreciates your kindness. I don't necessarily look at this as a bump in the road, but rather as an alternate route to the cure.

My doctor believes the PARP Inhibitors should have approval in the first quarter of 2011. I hope the FDA makes this happen for me and the other women this drug could help very soon!

Holding my head high and fighting like a cowgirl!
Sharyl

The Kindness of Family and Friends

Saturday, January 29, 2011

I started the new chemo drug on Thursday. Since it's taken in three-week cycles, my doctor will do another scan in nine weeks to check my progress. However, I did receive some very encouraging news on Friday. The cerebral spinal fluid test taken on Wednesday came back with a result of "rare atypical cells."

My nurse practitioner said this is good news since each test prior came back with a result of positive for canser. She feels that the conclusion from the last test means the cells are still canserous, but are clearing.

Canser can be such a lonely experience. I have a very supportive and loving network of family and friends, but the bottom line is that I am the only person who can take the drugs for me. I am the only one who can tolerate the pain of the headaches, vomiting and fatigue. And, I am the one who has to live inside my head deal with all of the what ifs. I was beginning to experience very serious sadness and loneliness and to feel like life is moving on without me.

But what I was reminded of today is how much people care and just want to help to take a little bit of the pain, the sadness and side effects away. I can't even begin to explain how overcome with emotion I became today when I went on our family's care calendar, which was started up again. My friend sent out an email on Thursday afternoon to let people know about helping out with a dinner due to my fatigue and headaches, and it is already full through April, and even for a couple of dinners in May.

My heart is filled with the beauty of the kindness of family and friends. It just helped lift my spirits and reminded me that there are so many helping hands extended to us during my treatment. Thank you, my friends. I fully plan to pay it forward in the future.

Thanks and God bless to all of you for reading my CaringBridge website, offering me words of encouragement and praying for me and my family. I am forever grateful.

Holding my head high and fighting like a cowgirl!

Love,
Sharyl

†

Sharyl,
You are the bravest and strongest woman I have ever had the honor of meeting. Your story, words of encouragement, strength and amazing attitude have taught me so much during this past year.

You are an incredible woman!
Ginny

Can I Get a YEEHAW?

Friday, February 11, 2011

At my chemo appointment on Tuesday, my nurse practitioner took out a sample of fluid to test for canser cells (the last four samples still showed atypical cells), and the fluid was a little bloody. When I came back on Thursday for my next injection, she started out by saying she was a little concerned about the bloody sample from the other day, and she wanted me to have a CT scan to make sure the port is still in the proper position.

I hate getting unexpectedly scanned. When she took the sample on Thursday, it was totally clear of any blood, making her think that the drug I get at the end of the week causes some inflammation, which can cause bloody samples. So, I thought I was off the hook for the CT because the sample wasn't bloody. But she popped her head back in the room and said, "I still want you to get a CT, so make sure you make an appointment before you leave." I was so annoyed because I started thinking about some of the what ifs...

This morning, I went in for the scan and the tech said they would have my results in a couple of days. I didn't expect the results before Monday simply because it was already 11:30 on Friday, but my phone rang at about 2:30 today, and it was my nurse practitioner. I really like her. We have a good relationship. We laugh and joke around while she is poking my head. She thinks we're nuts with all of this hockey stuff, and she has a great bedside manner.

She said the scan came back and everything looked good. The port was in the proper position. They could not see any of the canser cells in the fluid and then she said the results from my sample on Tuesday came back "CLEAR," which means the answer was "NO" for canser cells in the fluid. Can I get a "YEEHAW!?"

We are going to continue for a few more weeks with my current treatment schedule and then hopefully put some more time between treatments. I asked my nurse practitioner on Thursday if it would be okay if I had a glass of wine this weekend, and she said yes, as long as it was with her. When I talked to her today, I told her I was really going to enjoy my glass of wine tomorrow night! She said, "Please do!"

PRAISE GOD, PRAISE GOD, PRAISE GOD!!! (I learned at Abby's conference that in many writings you should use the power of three.) Thank you all for your prayers—they are working!

Holding my head high and fighting like a cowgirl. Have a great weekend.

Love,
Sharyl

†

Yeehaw, Sharyl!
I hope that I can celebrate with you and watch you enjoying your glass of wine! This *will* be a weekend to celebrate in more ways than one lady!

I look forward to spending some chilly time with you in the Hudson rinks and some drinks in the hotel!

Congrats, Sharyl! We are so happy for you!
Jen

Thank You to My Hockey Family

Tuesday, February 15, 2011

As many of you know, I'm very proud to be a member of the South St. Paul Community, and here is another reason why.

Last weekend, we spent Hockey Day Minnesota in Wisconsin. Both Jacob and Abby's teams were in the Hudson Mite and U8 Jamborees. Earlier in the season, my husband and brother Michael, who coach Abby's team, thought it would be a cool idea to have the U8 girls get pink and white jerseys with pink ribbons and the motto "Fight Like a Girl" on back. to wear at jamborees

Before the girls' first game started, they all gathered around the net, shouted "Sharyl!," raised their sticks, and then skated over to where I was sitting in the stands. It was so sweet to see all of their smiling eyes staring up at me. (Since they had their mouth guards in, their smiles were masked a little.)

Jacob's team wanted in on the action and so his team, along with another mite team, wore pink laces and taped their sticks with pink tape. Jacob's team also shouted my name at the net.

A bunch of the kids came up to me after their games and said, "Did you hear us shout your name?" Unfortunately, I didn't really understand what they were shouting, but they were so excited to see my reaction that I thought since I heard them shout (I just couldn't quite make out what they were saying), it's not really lying to say "Yes, I heard you."

My friend Jen, who is the U8 team manager, put together an article to submit to the Minnesota Youth Hockey Association *Let's*

Play Hockey newsletter that spoke to what our teams (players and parents) did in honor and support of our family, and I just want to send a huge thank you to my hockey family for your support and a great weekend.

Holding my head high and fighting like a cowgirl,
Sharyl

†

Sharyl,
What a beautiful, heartwarming story! It is a real story too! I love it! You touch so many people and everyone feels your warmth and down-to-earth, loving personality. You have the support of the entire community to beat this, and we are all here to help you and your family every step of the way! You are not alone!

God bless and keep fighting like a girl!
Kelli

Let's Play Hockey Article
Reprinted with Permission

February 17, 2010

South St. Paul (SSP) is located just south of Saint Paul and is a small, family friendly community situated on the banks of the Mississippi. SSP is known for its excellent school system, quality athletic programs, close knit neighborhoods, but more importantly, the people of South St. Paul are known for supporting each other.

This past weekend, the youth of SSP displayed their support for a cause near and dear to their hearts, the fight against breast cancer. As the SSP U8 girls and two boys' mite teams stepped on the ice at the Hudson Youth Hockey Jamboree, they dressed in pink and white in honor of dedicated hockey mom Sharyl Saver.

Sharyl, a mother, wife, sister, daughter, employee and community member was diagnosed with breast cancer in 2007. For the past four years, Sharyl has worked, participated in her children's events, volunteered, cooked, cleaned and tried to keep up with life, all while she continued chemotherapy and fought reccurrences of cancer. Through her strength and courage, Sharyl has taught the people of SSP how to take over the cancer and not let it overtake you.

Anyone associated with hockey knows the grueling schedules a family keeps when you have two children who play hockey, a husband that owns his own business, works as a firefighter, coaches his kids' teams, a son in college, plus school, religion and family time. For those of us not fighting cancer, the demands of life can pile up.

As a community and hockey association, friends and family have stepped in to help the Saver family continue life, enjoy each other and take the things we are capable of helping with off of Jason and Sharyl's plate. The community members deliver meals twice a week, friends assist with carpooling the children to and from school and practices, hockey moms help clean and keep up the house, and for the days when rest is the best thing for Sharyl, the hockey families videotape her children's games, so that she doesn't miss seeing them play. As much as the community does to help, the reality is that Sharyl is the only one who can take the medication, get the chemo and fight the disease.

As a surprise to Sharyl, her husband Jason and brother Michael had pink and white jerseys with the breast cancer ribbons on the sleeve created by iJersey. They had Sharyl's motto, "Fight Like a Girl" put on the back of the jersey. The U8 girls' team, which Sharyl's daughter Abby plays on, purchased the jerseys to wear at the jamboree. A portion of the proceeds from the jerseys sold go to the Susan G. Komen for the Cure foundation. The jerseys were such a hit that even girls who don't play on the team and their mothers purchased them as well.

Jacob Saver, Sharyl's youngest son, wanted his team to do something to show their support, too. He came up with the idea to have his team and the other mite team wear pink laces, tape their sticks with pink tape, and wear breast-cancer ribbons on their helmets. As a youth association, the goal was to show Sharyl our love and support and to show everyone else that even children can take a stand against this life-affecting disease.

Besides the profit from "Fight Like a Girl" jersey orders, the three SSP teams had a "Coins for Change" bucket passed during the games. For each goal scored this weekend, people contributed coins to the bucket and all money donated will be sent to Susan G. Komen for the Cure for breast cancer research in honor of Sharyl.

There were many game victories, but the most important victory was the raising of approximately $700 to be donated to a cause worth "Fighting Like a Girl" for!

Congratulations to the youth and families for making a difference in the world!

Angels Among Us

There Is Always Room for Hope and Miracles

Tuesday, March 22, 2011

The other day, I heard a promo for the show "The Doctors" that really caught my attention. Dr. Travis Stork, an ER doctor and one of the show's hosts, said "There is no such thing as a terminal diagnosis." He further explained that the reason he believes this is because we never know what's going to happen. There are always new treatments on the horizon. He also said it is their job to give the patient and their families the facts, but there is always room for hope and miracles.

About two weeks ago, I had an MRI of the fluid around my brain. Friday, March 11th, my nurse practitioner said my breast canser tumor markers had dropped in half in just one month. She was so excited, she had to share the news with me right away.

She didn't have the results of the MRI yet. Later that day, one of the nurses from the clinic called and said my nurse practitioner wanted me to know she got the results of the MRI, and the scan showed great results. It wasn't totally clear, but the original spots are very light or gone.

Turns out the bloody sample from a while back gave a false report of being clear of the atypical cells. But the cell counts in the fluid are down, and the MRI showed that the treatments are working. So, I will continue on with my current treatment with twice weekly injections.

Yesterday, I had a PET scan to monitor the other areas of my body and to measure the effectiveness of a new chemotherapy drug I'm on. My nurse practitioner again very excitedly wanted to share the news with me that the PET scan showed a significant decrease in the liver metastases and most of the lymph-node lighting is gone. Just those pesky ones under my arm but my arm is swollen from lymphodema, which I think is why they continue to light up.

I am going to continue on the new oral drug and am happy about that since if it had gotten worse, they were going to switch me to a drug that causes hair loss. Vain, I know, but my hair is growing so fast, and I am really starting to like the dark hair growing out of my head. Yet I will always be a blonde at heart.

My hair is kind of thin, but I hope to go wigless more often as soon as it warms up. And, since I won't be able to color my hair, I can always take advantage of my blonde wigs.

More good news. It has been about four weeks since I've had a headache. As a result, I feel a lot better. I have more energy and don't spend most of my days in bed anymore.

Thank you for your prayers, for the meals and restaurant certificates, the monthly cleaning and the cards of encouragement. We have so many special people in our life, and we are grateful for every one of you. I am thankful each day that I get to spend here on Earth and share my life with my family and friends. God bless.

Holding my head high and fighting like a cowgirl,
Sharyl

God's Love and Devotion

*But thanks be to God, who in Christ always leads us
in triumphal procession, and through us spreads
the fragrance of the knowledge of Him everywhere.*
—2 Corinthians 2:14

Dear Mom,

Thank you for raising me as a Christian and introducing me to God's love, beauty, blessings, kindness, compassion and hope.

You have always been a source of inspiration to me with your dedication to your husband and children. You have set an excellent and long-lasting example of unconditional love that I can now demonstrate and pass on to my children.

You are a beautiful woman, both inside and out. I am so thankful and blessed that you are my mother; You are a gift to your family. I thank you and Dad for the love you have for each other and it is by your relationship that each one of your children have been blessed with loving spouses and fulfilling marriages. That gift to us and to you and Dad is not by accident; it was made possible by your prayers and the loving marriage you and Dad share.

I pray that you are filled with peace, love, joy and enlightenment of God's love and devotion to you, a wonderful child of God. May your love for the Father be deepened and strengthened as you discuss, share and fellowship the gift He gave to us all, Jesus Christ, his son who died in order that we would have eternal life.

I love you and you are in my daily thoughts and prayers,
Sharyl

God Bless to All of You

Thursday, May 12, 2011

Thanks and God bless to all of you reading my CaringBridge website, offering me words of encouragement and praying for me and my family. I am forever grateful. I'm sorry it has been quite some time since I've updated. For the most part, I have felt good. I had an MRI last Wednesday. Everything on the MRI looked great. No new lesions. Stay the course...

Last Thursday, I went to the doctor. My legs were wobbly but nothing major. She suggested continuing to use a cane. Saturday, I woke up, and I couldn't walk. I could not stand to put pressure on my legs. So, poor Jason had to pick me up drag me around the house because I just couldn't get my legs to move around when I wanted them to go somewhere. It was very frustrating.

I had a doctor's appointment on Wednesday, and she wanted me admitted to the hospital so that I could have another MRI because of the paralysis. They got me admitted, and we sat and we sat and we sat. Finally, we were told my room was ready. However, we couldn't get anyone to approve the MRI. Finally at 9 p.m. (we got there at 2 p.m.) we got an approval, and I went in for a two-hour MRI. I was exhausted at the end of it. You wouldn't think...just lying around...

They were looking to see if the canser had spread to the spine. I kind of suspected it had not. This morning the chief of neurology came and said there was nothing to indicate canser cells had spread to the spine and that I most likely am having a nerve reaction to an infection of some sort.

So my nurse practitioner is going to come help use my port to centrifuge the immunoglobulin therapy to treat this (you'll never believe it) rare disorder! The nurse practitioner is coming here because nobody else wants to touch it. She's kind of a renegade so she loves this stuff! (It sounds much more cowgirl than it needs to.) Anyway, the sooner I get started, the sooner I can get out of here.

Holding my head high and fighting like a cowgirl!

Love,
Sharyl

†

Sharyl,

Over the years, I have read your inspiring words. It's been like reading the greatest novel ever written. I've pulled strength and reverence from your words when I have needed them.

I know it's God and God alone who keeps us grounded. He has been at your side and is holding you in His comfortable arms each and every day. Thank you for the words you write.

Blessings to you and your family,
Sis

Home with My Family

Saturday, May 28, 2011

I have been trying to update for two and a half days. I'm having some trouble, but I am bound and determined to get something out this evening.

Anyway, I have shared with you all over the last couple of years how much I enjoy reality TV. The other evening, I watched The Biggest Loser results show contestants waiting for their turns to weigh in. I was so genuinely excited and moved for them.

See, I always felt in a way it was sort of easy for them because they had health professionals watching their every move. And, if you just get your weight affairs in order there are so many ways to reclaim your health. You can reverse diabetes, heart disease and so on if you just take better care of yourself; I am aware it is not that simple, but it's a start to making life better for them.

Anyway, as each contestant weighed in, I was simply and genuinely overjoyed for their amazing accomplishments.

My thoughts are a little jumbled today since it has been such a long two weeks, but the best thing is that I am at home with my family. I am sitting next to the basement walk-out door, with the amazing breeze on my face and truly feeling how amazingly blessed I am at the moment. I hope you all have a wonderful weekend.

Thank you all for your love and support.

Holding my head high and fighting like a cowgirl!
Sharyl

Angels Among Us

He who dwells in the shelter of the Most High
will rest in the shadow of the Almighty.
I will say of the Lord "He is my refuge and my fortress,
my God, in whom I trust
—Psalm 91: 1-2

Friday, June 17, 2011

In the spirit of Sharyl referring to her caregivers as her "Posse," this is some of "Sharyl's Posse" writing to give you an update. We would like to bring you up-to-speed on what has been going on in Sharyl and her family's life.

Last Saturday, June 11th, the crew from Jason's fire house, Station 4, surprised them by bringing three rigs and 10 firefighters to their house to deliver good wishes, love and support, along with a very generous donation.

It did raise curiosity among the neighbors at first, but Jason reassured everyone it was just his firefighter family showing their support for Jason, Sharyl and the kids. On behalf of the family, we would like to say a huge thank you to the firefighters of St. Paul for all you have done and continue to do for Jason and the family.

We also would like to say thank you to all who have shown your love and support in so many ways. Whether bringing meals, taking the kids places, visiting with Sharyl, walking Blazer, sending flowers or offering your love and support through prayer. All of these acts speak volumes to us as they show how much Sharyl is loved by so many.

We also want to thank those who have volunteered to spend hours with Sharyl for her day-to-day care so that Jason can run his errands, take the kids to their games and try to maintain a normal life. God has truly blessed Sharyl with so many loving and caring family members and friends, and she loves you all.

You ALL are Angels Among Us.

To everyone who has shown support for Sharyl through family or friendship and the many people who support Sharyl through these connections, your love, support and prayers, are greatly appreciated.

As far as the day to day, Sharyl is sleeping a lot but does perk up when someone in the house is talking and likes to include her thoughts in the conversation. She also smiles and her eyes twinkle when someone new comes by. Her appetite is not quite what it was, but she is still eating.

Since Sharyl is not progressing as well as we hoped, the physical and occupational therapists will no longer be coming to work with her. We will continue to do range of motion, moving her from side to side and getting her into the wheelchair, when possible. She did have chemo on June 8th and is scheduled for another treatment on June 22nd, providing her blood counts are good.

While Sharyl continues to fight like a cowgirl, we ask that you continue to lift Sharyl and her family in your prayers, believing in her cowgirl spirit.

God bless you all,
Sharyl's Posse

†

Sharyl,

I can't help but think of you when I think things are a little difficult and manage to whine about it. But thinking of you puts a STOP sign up, saying, "Pick your chin up, smile and move forward!"

I think you have been a teacher to a lot of folks. A teacher of inspiration. A teacher of love. A teacher of courage. A teacher of faith. A teacher of grace. A teacher of humor (love your laugh!). A teacher of optimism. A teacher who stays in the minds of people whose lives you continue to touch every day.

The following seems to sum up for me what I can learn from you: Facing adversity while holding your head high is really the only way to go about it in this life.

I am praying God holds you and your family tightly in His arms.

Indian Serenity Prayer: *"God, grant me the strength of eagle wings, the faith and courage to fly to new heights, and the wisdom to rely on His spirit to carry me there."*

We love you...always.
Darin

God's Rainbow Is Coming

Wednesday, June 22, 2011

This past Thursday and Friday, Abby performed in her dance recital and she danced so beautifully, looking so much like her mother did for so many years. Sharyl was unable to attend but did watch a video of her later.

On Saturday, Taylor celebrated his 22nd birthday and on Sunday, Sharyl and Jason celebrated their 12th wedding anniversary, as well as Father's Day. It was also a day spent with her whole family, which has always been important to Sharyl.

Now the time has come for Sharyl to move into the next phase of her journey. She will be under the care of Hospice and continue at home, surrounded by all who love her.

> *"I called on your name, LORD, from the depths of the pit. You heard my plea: "Do not close your ears to my cry for relief." You came near when I called you, and you said, "Do not fear."*
> —Lamentations 3: 55-57

Sharyl indeed called on the Lord in her time of trouble and He heard her call, and He comforted her. He gave her strength, courage and hope when she needed it. This does not mean that Sharyl's fighting spirit was for nothing or that she has given up. It is just a change in course.

Her "Fight Like a Girl" and "Cowgirl" attitudes have been an inspiration to so many over the past two years and she can continue to be that inspiration as she puts herself in the loving arms of her Lord and Savior, the true healer. We ask that you continue to lift Sharyl and her family in prayers as they take this journey together.

Sharyl has always had a fondness for rainbows, so we would say to you now, remember the rainbow. God has promised us that when we come to Him in prayer, He will listen. He will never leave us. He will comfort us and give us peace. We can think of no more beautiful example of God's promise to us than the rainbow.

> *Rainbows appear after mighty storms,*
> *When things look their very worst,*
> *Just when the skies are darkest gray,*
> *Look for the rainbow first.*
> *The rainbow is a sign of God's promise,*
> *That He will guide us through any storm,*
> *That He will see us through all our troubles,*
> *No matter what their form.*
> *When you feel battered by life's storms,*
> *And you are filled with doubt and dismay;*
> *Just remember God's rainbow is coming*
> *It's only a prayer away.*

—*Unknown*

God bless you all for keeping Sharyl's cowgirl spirit in your hearts,
Sharyl's Posse

✝

Sharyl, Jason, Taylor, Jacob and Abby,

I hope you feel God's love (and mine too) as you travel on this next journey. Even though I am not there physically, my arms are tightly around you, and I am here to hold you up if you need it, to listen to you if you need to talk and to just hug and love you when you need that too. Your entire family is so special to me, and I am honored to have you in my life.

Sharyl, you have taught me so much, and I owe you so very much for letting me travel this journey with you. I will never look at rainbows or butterflies in the same way, and I will always believe that no matter what life throws my way, I can fight like a cowgirl too. Thank you for being my friend and showing me how to be strong and courageous.

My thoughts and prayers are with you tonight, tomorrow and every tomorrow after that! I hope you feel the peace and love that you so deserve!

God bless you!
Mary

Fly to Jesus and Live!

*My Father's house has many rooms; if that were not so,
would I have told you that I am going there to prepare a place for you?
And if I go and prepare a place for you, I will come back and take you
to be with me that you also may be where I am.*
—John 14: 2-3

Wednesday, July 6, 2011

Our beloved and precious Sharyl Lynn (Stanefski) Saver has gone home to be with Jesus and reunited with her sweet Caylin and other family members who are waiting to greet her. Sharyl was a loving wife, mother, daughter, sister, aunt, niece, cousin, daughter-in-law, sister-in-law, friend and co-worker.

For four years, as Sharyl took on this thing called canser, her cowgirl attitude and fighting spirit were an inspiration to all who faithfully followed her CaringBridge journal entries. Canser may have ended her life, but it could not take the life from her spirit as she lived each day with hope and love.

Sharyl loved life and all that life could bring. She had an infectious laugh, and you couldn't help but laugh with her. She loved going to her cabin and being outdoors. She loved sports, both participating and watching. She was an avid Twins fan, but mostly loved watching her children in their sporting activities.

She loved exercising, lifting weights, doing aerobics and running. (She ran the 5k at the Susan G. Komen Race for the Cure with her brother Michael the first year after her initial diagnosis and took third place in the survivor category.) She loved music and dancing, listening to her brother's band (their #1 fan) and especially listening to her son Taylor play his guitar and sing.

Sharyl loved people, including her many special friends. She loved her family, not just her immediate family, but also her whole extended family. She loved her aunts and uncles, cousins, nieces and nephews and her in-laws. She loved her brother and sisters deeply and had a very close and special relationship with each of them. She loved her dad. He was her knight in shining armor, her hero. She loved her mother, her encourager, confidante and friend.

Sharyl loved her children. Her precious Caylin and sweet Abigail, her little man Jacob and Taylor, her oldest, tallest but always her little boy. Her children were her pride and joy, and she cherished each one of them.

And, of course, she loved her husband Jason. He was her prince charming, soul mate, lover and best friend. He could always make her laugh, no matter what the situation, as he would remind her that there is so much more to life than canser. His positive attitude helped her to always see the sunshine instead of the rain, as together they looked for the rainbow.

Sharyl also loved the Lord. It was this love and faith in God that gave her the strength and courage to travel this journey with so much hope. Sharyl understood that being a child of God is not an insurance policy against all the trials, dangers and even death that is a part of this world. But because she put her faith and trust in God, she knew He would always hold her close and His great love would carry her through all circumstances.

As much as Sharyl loved, she also was loved by so many. So we say Thank You and God bless to ALL of you who were there for her in so many ways as she fought like a cowgirl. Your love and support meant so much to Sharyl, as well as to her family.

We will miss you, Sharyl, and your beautiful smile and contagious laugh, but we take hope in the fact that we will see you again. Until then, we say farewell.

Fly to Jesus and Live!

A Symbol of Hope

A butterfly lights beside us like a sunbeam

And for a brief moment its glory

and beauty belong to our world

But then it flies again

And though we wish it could have stayed

We feel lucky to have seen it.

Acknowledgments

Sharyl had an amazing gift for putting words together on paper in a way that moved and inspired others. Encouraged by many of her faithful CaringBridge followers, Sharyl dreamed of writing a book.

"For I know the plans I have for you," declares the Lord," plans to prosper you and not to harm you, plans to give you hope and a future."
—Jeremiah 29:11

Sharyl trusted in the plans the Lord had for her and placed her hope and future in His hands. We believe God still has plans for Sharyl's writings.

Discussions with her friend Leah Galle were the motivating factor in bringing *Fight with Cowgirl Spirit* to publication. We extend our appreciation to Leah for her dedicated work on the book and website and to Liina Lundin of Liina Lundin Graphic Design for creating the beautiful book cover and website graphics.

We thank God for bringing these women together to help fulfill Sharyl's dream. We also extend our gratitude to family near and far, her loyal CaringBridge followers, faithful prayer warriors, medical team and many friends and co-workers for supporting and encouraging Sharyl throughout her journey.

Finally, thank you to CaringBridge Inc. for providing the website platform that made it possible for Sharyl to share her story. We are forever grateful.

—Sharyl's Posse